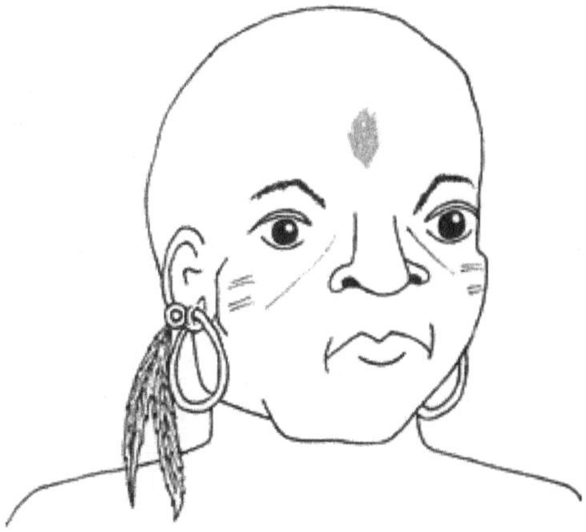

Book Of Mormon Puzzle Pages

by Elizabethe Walto

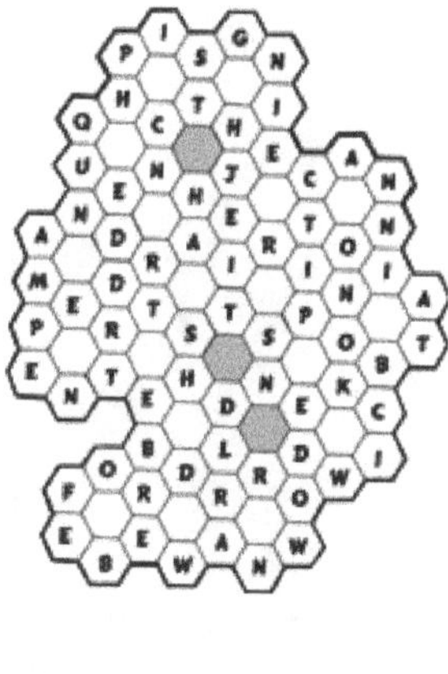

Published by Walton Publishing
213 W. Main St.
Palmyra NY 14522

January 2017, revised June 2017

Book of Mormon Puzzle Pages, Volume 1

ISBN 978-1-62039-011-5

This Puzzle book is designed to enhance personal and family study of the Book of Mormon on a daily basis. The puzzles vary in difficulty from very easy to quite challenging, but on the challenging pages there are pictures to color so that even very young children can color and participate.

It is my hope that this will make study of the Book of Mormon more enjoyable and meaningful.

Feedback is welcome: BoMpuzzles@dbwalton.com

Please check out our website at BomPuzzles.com

Dedicated to my very patient husband, Brent Walton, who has been so supportive of the many hours and late nights involved as I put this book together!

Book of Mormon Puzzle Pages

Volume 1 - Puzzles List

0. The Book of Mormon Has Many Names
1. Nephi Made a Record
2. Lehi Sees a Vision
3. Lehi Preaches
4. Laman and Lemuel Were Unhappy
4b. Leaving Jerusalem
5. Nephi Is Different
5b. Nephi Prays
6. Nephi Had Faith
7. Wicked Laban
7b. An Angel Appears
8. Nephi Slay Laban
9. Nephi Convinces Zoram
10. My Sons Are Back!
11. Of Great Worth
12. Rebellion!
13. Nephi Is Freed
14. Tree of Life
15. Lehi's Vision
16. Making Plates
17. Lehi Prophesies of the Messiah
18. The Olive Tre
19. The Iron Rod
20. The Meaning of the Tree
21. The Good Shepherd
22. Twelve Nephite Disciples
23. The Great Divide
24. The Many Waters
25. A Record of the Jews
26. These Things Shall Come Forth
27. One Shepherd
28. Two Churches Only
29. He Shall Write
29b. Concerning the End of the World
30. Nephi Prays for Knowledge
31. A Branch of Israel
32. Nephi's Brothers Ask Him
33. Nephi Exhorts His Brethren
34. The Liahona
35. Finding Game
36. Camel Travel
37. Building the Ship
38. Rude Brothers
39. God's Lovely Creation
40. Touch Me Not
41. Nephi Builds a Ship
41b. Sailing to the Promised Land
42. A Bad Storm
43. Book of Mormon Animals
44. I Had Made These Plates
45. The Crucifixion
46. Likening the Scriptures
47. Peace Like A River
48. The Prophet Isaiah
49. Nephi Quotes Isaiah
50. Scattered Israel
51. Queens Thy Nursing Mothers
52. Future Days
53. Jerusalem is Destroyed
54. Lehi Blesses His Children
55. Shake Off Those Chains
56. Authority
57. The Light of Christ
58. Opposition In All Things
59. Men Are That They Might Have Joy
60. Joseph and Joseph
61. Two Sticks
62. A Promise to the Lamanites
63. My Soul Delighteth
64. Psalm of Nephi
65. Lamanites and Nephites
66. Nephi's People Prosper
67. Consecrated Brothers
68. Kings Thy Nursing Fathers
69. The Messiah Will Come
70. I Will Comfort Her Waste Places
71. They Shall Come to Zion
72. He Will Come In the Body
73. The Spirit and the Body
74. Day of Judgment
75. The Atonement Satisfieth

Puzzle Solutions Follow

The Book of Mormon Has Been Given Many Names

Can you find these phrases in the wordchains in the squares?
Words can go up, down, right or left, but NOT diagonally.
One is already done for you as an example.

Find:
A Voice from the Dust
The Golden Plates
Record of Our Fathers
Book of Mormon
Stick of Joseph
Gold Bible
The Word of God

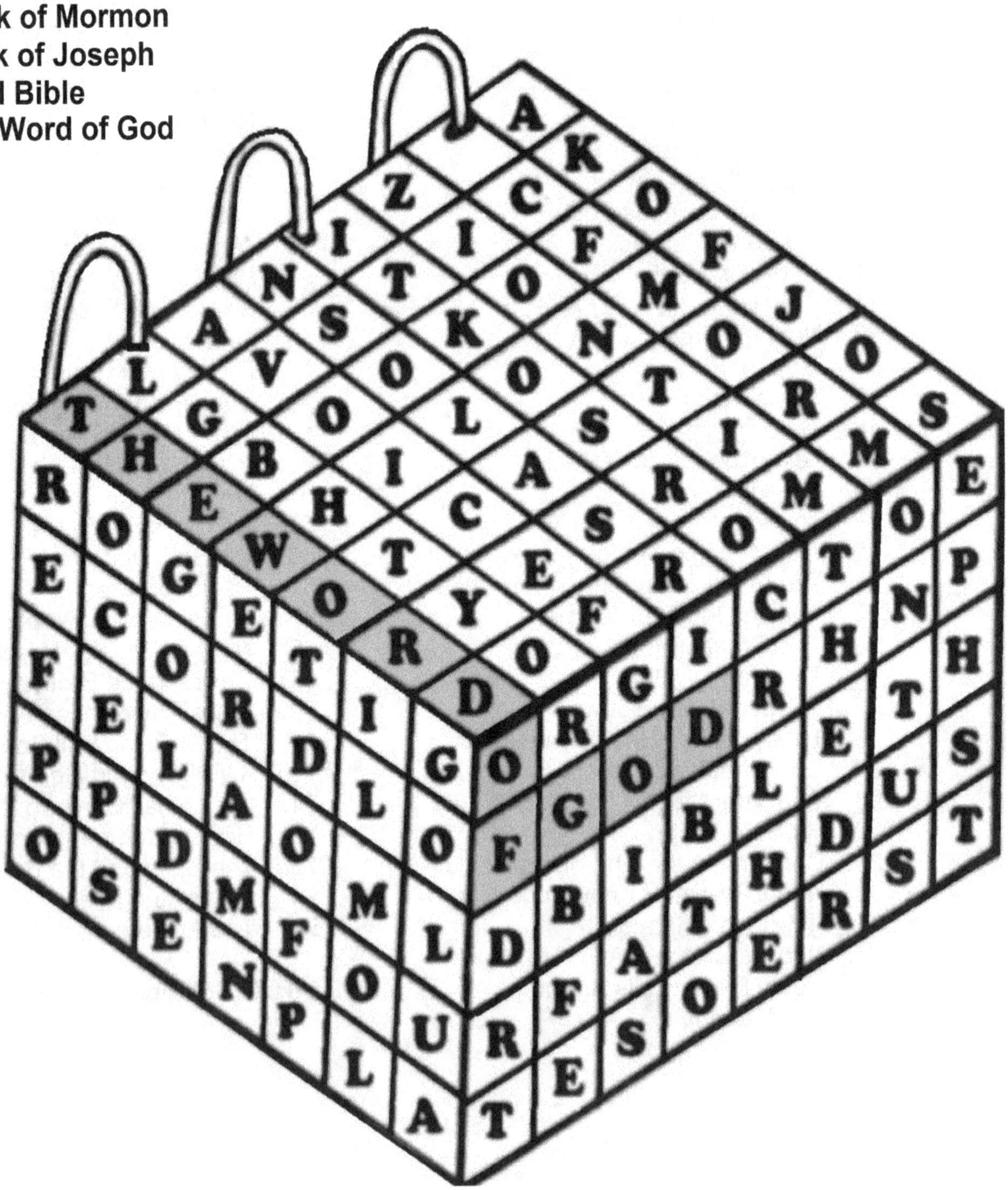

Nephi Made a Record

Can you help Nephi find his way to the record?

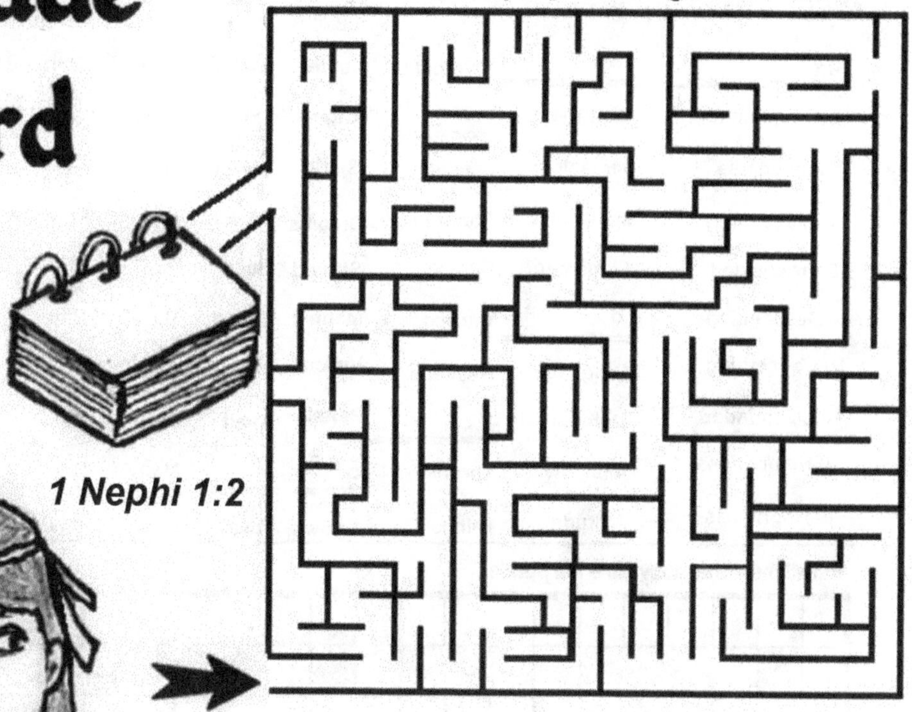

(Can you figure out the code for Nephi's journal?)

LEHI SEES IN A VISION THE DESTRUCTION OF JERUSALEM

1 Nephi 1:13

10+	9	Overcome	Luster	Sword	Book	With	God	Of		
12 Abominations	Destroyed	7	Angels	Thine	Thus	Read	Sun	On	Wo	To
11 Inhabitants	Jerusalem	Himself	Spirit	Mercy	When	Cast	Who	So	He	Do
11 Exceedingly	Marvelous	Thought	Dreams	Power	Wilt	High	Has		It	Heard
10 Prophesied	Firmament	Captive	Should	Heart	Fire	3	Own			
10 Descending	8	Carried	Manner	Stood	Have	Had	Not			
10 Concerning	Language	Heavens	Vision	Thine	Seen	Bed	Out			
10 Surrounded	Merciful	6	Perish	Shalt	Also	Did	2			
10 Numberless	Almighty	Throne	5	4	Many	One	In			
10 Brightness	Attitude	Things	Shown	Away	Such	Saw	At			

Put all the words above into the puzzle

LEHI PREACHES TO THE PEOPLE OF JERUSALEM

Fit all the underlined words into the puzzle. Once you have them in correctly, the circled letters will spell another word that is fairly important to Jerusalem's future.

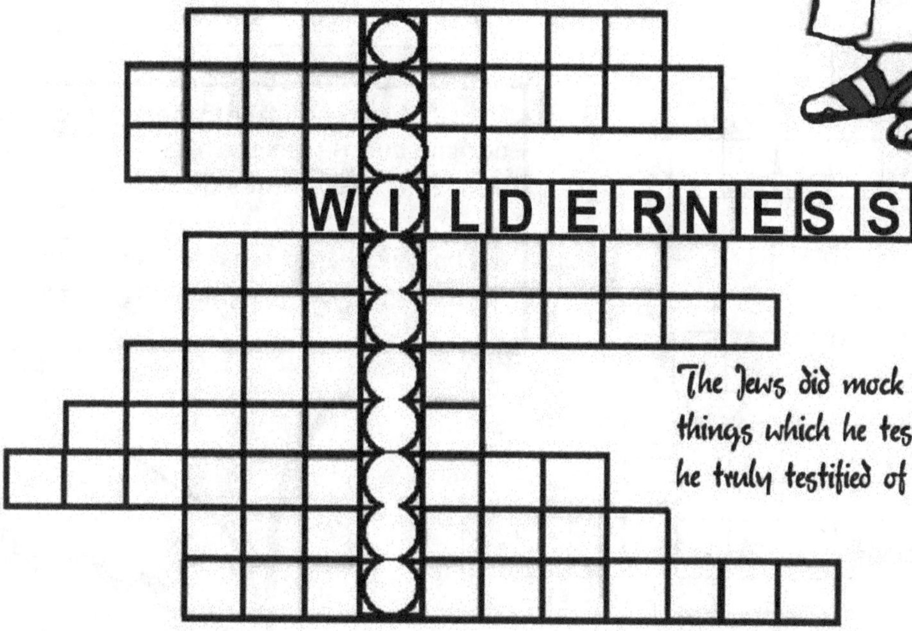

The Jews did mock him because of the things which he testified of them for he truly testified of their wickedness.

1 Nephi 1:19

Lehi was obedient and began to prophesy to the people concerning their wickedness and abominations and future destruction. He told them of the marvelous plan of redemption of the world by the coming Messiah. He told them to be faithful, but they sought to kill him. God then told Lehi to depart into the wilderness with his family, leaving behind their precious things and the land of their inheritance.

Laman and Lemuel Were Unhappy

They did not want to leave their homes and their friends and their precious things and hey did not believe in the prophecies of their father or that Jerusalem was wicked. They were like the people from Jerusalem who wanted to kill their father.

From the letters in the spiral, fill in the blanks below to see what was their problem

M	E	H	T	D	E	T	A	E	R
D	E	H	T	T	O	N	W	E	C
E	U	M	D	I	D	Y	E	N	D
A	R	M	U	R	B	E	H	K	A
L	I	N	G	S	O	C	T	Y	H
					F	A	↑	E	O
					T	U		H	H
					H	S	E	T	W
					A	T	G	O	D

1 Nephi 2:12

Their father, Lehi, talked to them and encouraged them to be righteous. He named a river, Laman, and a valley, Lemuel, after them to help them. **1 Nephi 2: 9-10**

But finally he had to speak to them with power from the Spirit which "shook their frames" so that they obeyed him

STUBBORNESS!

Packing Up the Camels

God told Lehi that the city would be destroyed. He and his family left on camels with tents. Can you help them pack?

1 Nephi 2:5

Can you fit all the names of the family into the crossword?

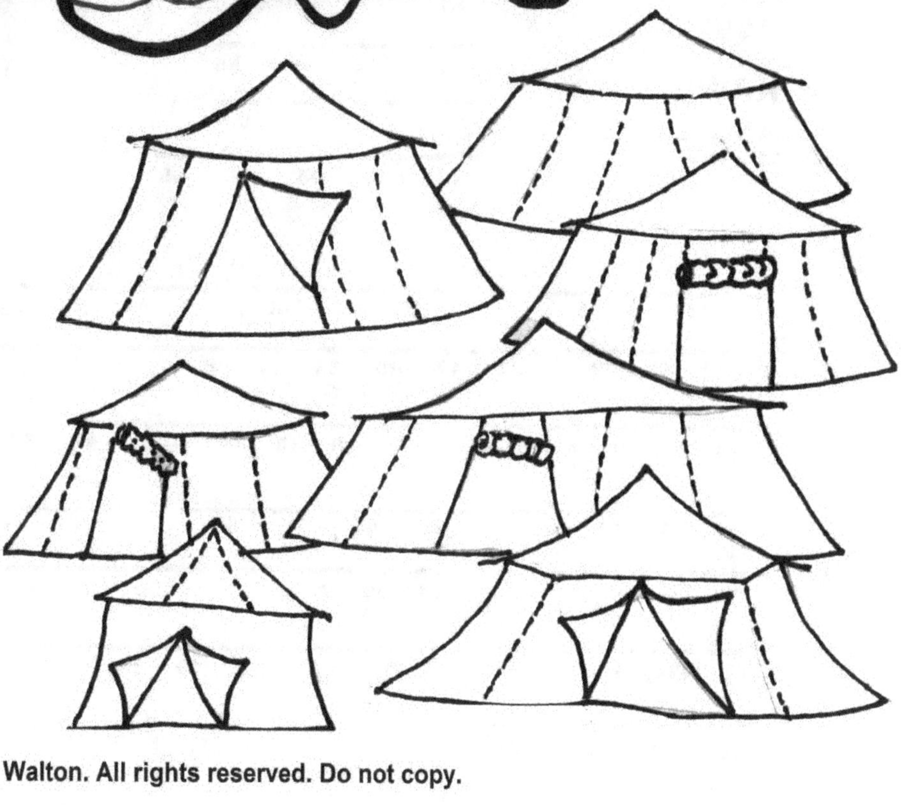

NEPHI IS DIFFERENT FROM HIS BROTHERS

Behold I Nephi will show unto you that

the tender mercies of the Lord are over all whom he hath chosen, because of their faith, to make them mighty even unto the power of deliverance.

1 Nephi 1:20

Nephi was:

GUNYO: 1 2 3 4 5

NEETBODI: 6 7 8 9 10 11 12 13

GROSTN: 14 15 16 17 18 19

HEBLUM: 20 21 22 23 24 25

TUFFHILA: 26 27 28 29 30 31 32 33

TAILVAN: 34 35 36 37 38 39 40

Laman and Lemuel were:

HESSFLI: 41 42 43 44 45 46 47

LUCRE: 48 49 50 51 52

ZAYL: 53 54 55 56

KAWE: 57 58 59 60

UDROP: 61 62 63 64 65

15 47 58 | J 25 57 46 | 9 45 9 | 22 17 48 60

47 45 22 | 23 42 48 54 64 46 42 | 63 44 | 13 47 58

40 30 28 18 19 41 | 57 20 10 48 20 | 47 42

13 11 41 29 10 26 45 51 65 | 17 31

40 20 8 22 ------ 54 39 9 | 29 20 51 1

27 52 14 2 | 41 63 64 19 47 13 | 47 10 14

43 28 44 58

Nephi Prays to Understand

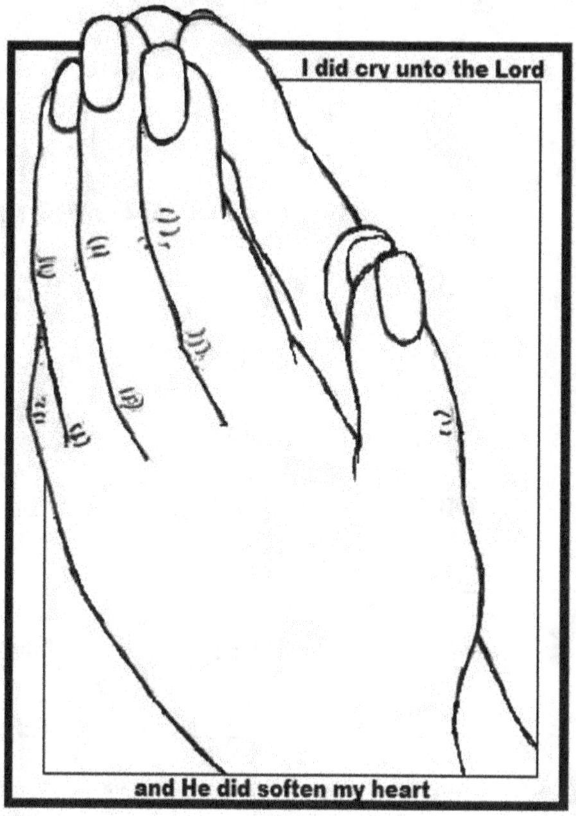

1 Nephi 2:20

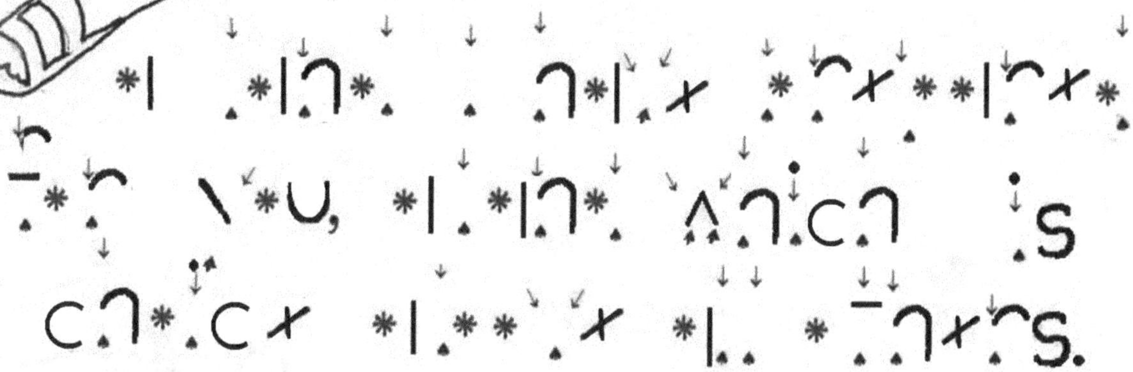

When you see a like this * put a circle this size ◯ around it like this! ⊛

When you see a mark like this ✗ put a partial circle around it like this! C

When you see an arrow like this → draw a line until you come to a stop like this! •

Now can you figure out what the puzzle says?

Nephi Had Faith

I _ I _ _   _ O   A _ _   _ O

_ _ E   _ _ I _ _ _   _ _ I _ _   _ _ E

_ O _ _   _ A _ _   _ O _ _ A _ _ E _

_ O _   I   _ _ O _   _ _ A _   _ _ E

_ O _ _   _ I _ E _ _   _ O

_ O _ _ A _ _ _ E _ _ _   U _ _ O

_ _ E   _ _ I _ _ _ E _   O _   _ E _

_ A _ E   _ E   _ _ E _ A _ E _ _   A

_ A _   _ O _   _ _ E _   _ _ A _

_ _ E _   _ A _   A _ _ O _ _ _ I _ _

_ _ E   _ _ I _ _   _ _ I _ _   _ E

_ O _ _ A _ _ E _ _   _ _ E _.

Can you figure out what Nephi is saying? The vowels are there for you, but you will have to figure out the consonants by counting how many there are:

K – 1	V – 2	F – 2
G – 3	Y – 3	P – 3
D – 10	M – 12	N - 12
S – 5	W -5	L – 8
C – 8	T – 17	H – 25
R - 7		

Wicked Laban Stole Their Precious Things!

1 Nephi 3:25

Can you help the brothers find their way to Laban's house in Jerusalem? You need to go by their house and pick up their precious things, and you need to avoid Laban's servants, too.

Often, it is when we have tried everything that we know how to do that Heavenly Father steps in to make a way for us. But he wants us to try our hardest first!

An Angel Appears

The angel asks two questions of Nephi's brothers:

To find out the first question, start with the second letter and select every other letter.

To find out the second question, start with the first letter and select every other letter, then add "you."

Write your answers here:

1

2

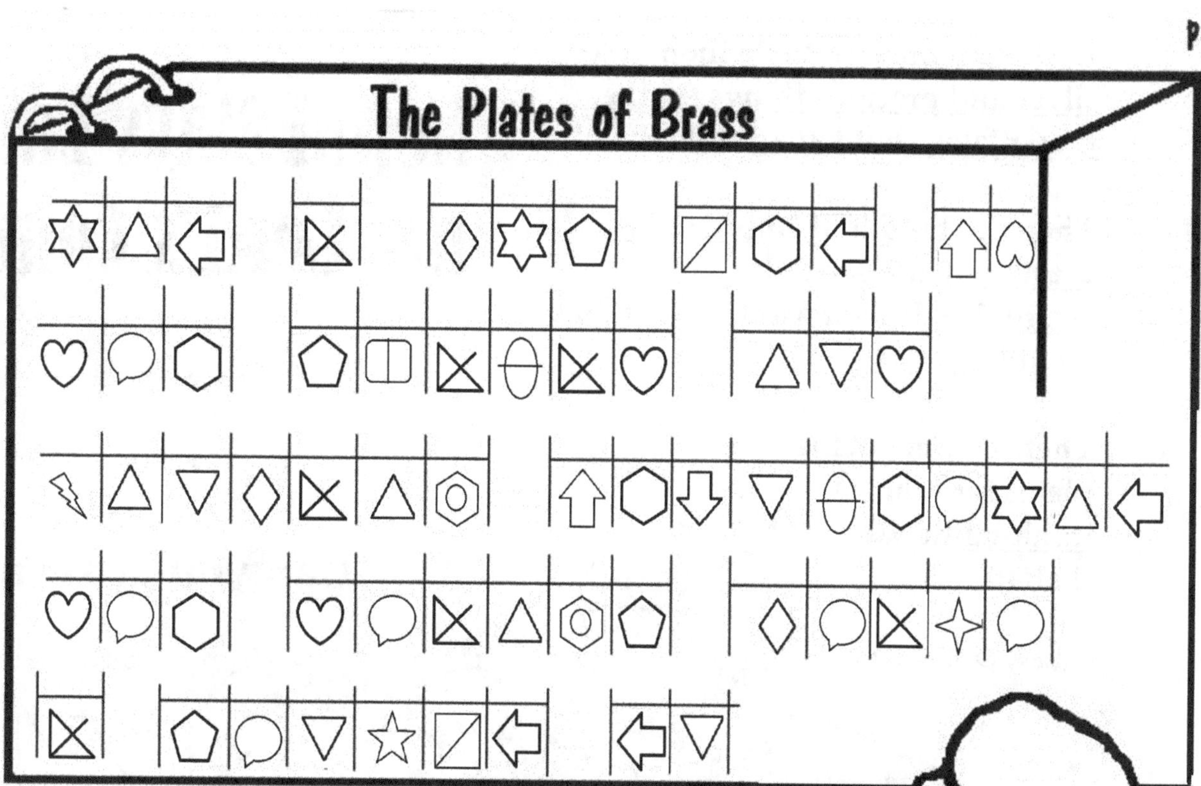

A Record of Great Worth

Can you figure out the code with the following clues?

1 Nephi 4:6 and 13

H is the most common consonant
I is the most common vowel
There are only 3 of W
There are only 2 of B, G, R and L
There are only one of Y and C and F
The symbols below are vowels:

There is only one U, K
and only one P,

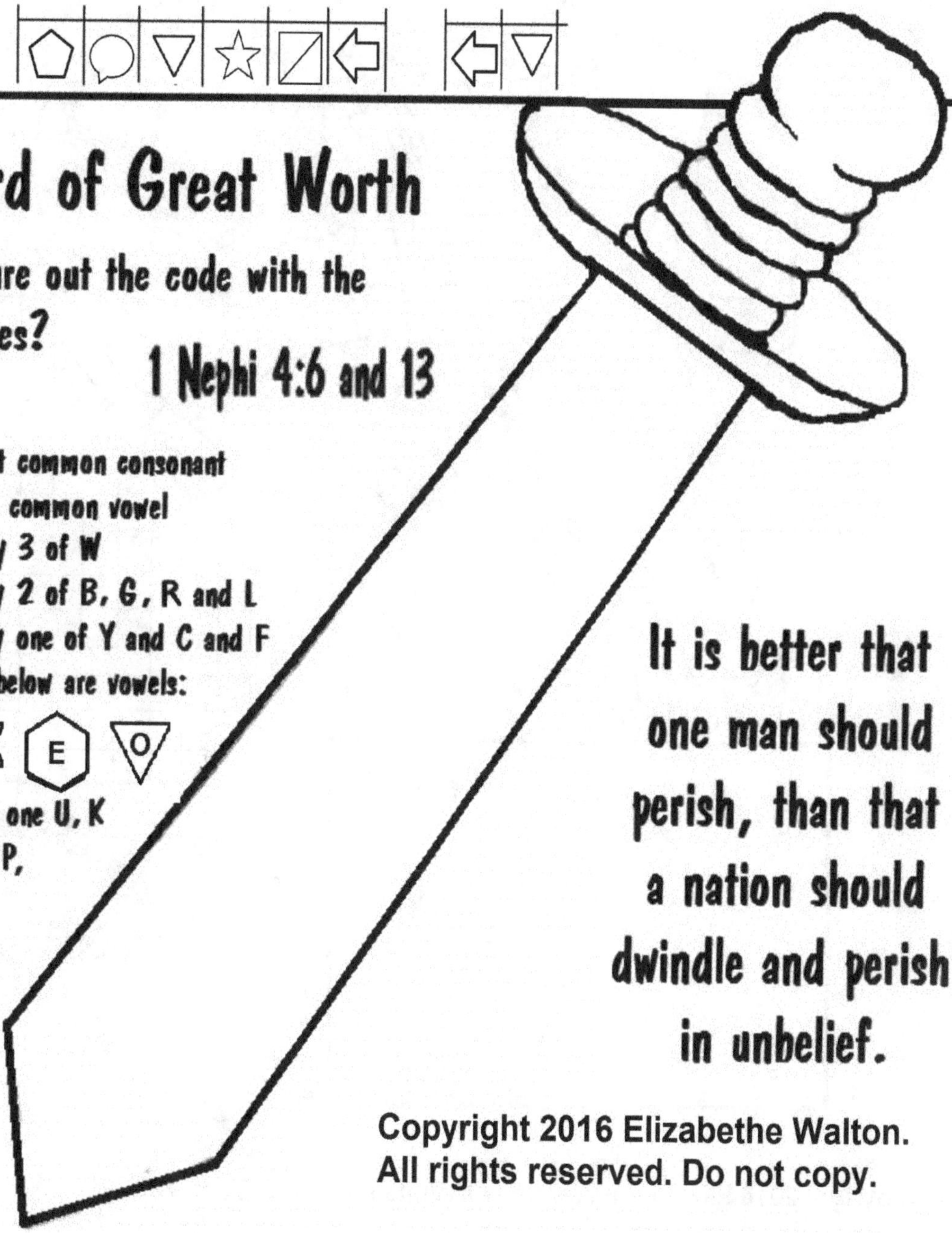

It is better that one man should perish, than that a nation should dwindle and perish in unbelief.

Nephi Slays Laban at the Lord's Command

First, they tried to trade their gold, silver and precious things for the brassplates, but Laban stole them!

Then the Lord told Nephi to kill drunken Laban with his own sword. He did not want to do it, but he did..

Then Zoram got the plates for him, thinking he was Laban.

1 Nephi 4:10

Can you draw a sword?

Put the underlined words into the puzzle

Nephi Convinces Zoram to Join Them

Sariah Rejoices

PLATES OF GREAT WORTH

> The plates of brass ...of great worth to us, insomuch that we could preserve the commandments of the Lord unto our children

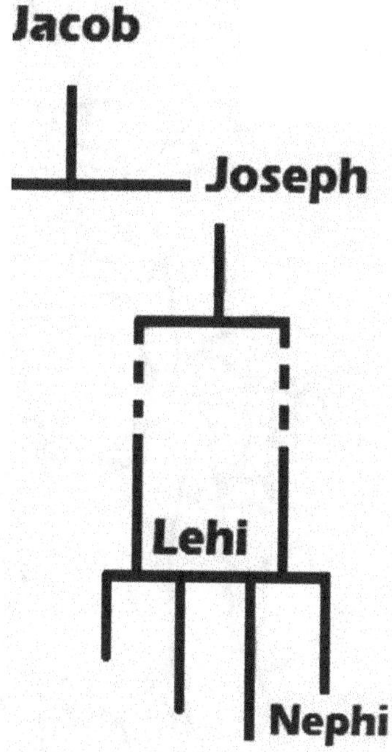

- The country ___ where Joseph was a slave
- Lehi found he was a ___ of Joseph
- A man who ___ had the brass plates in Jerusalem
- The king of Judah in ___ Lehi's time
- ___ Nephi's mother
- Nephi's oldest brother ___
- The ball that ___ God gave to the Nephites
- ___ A heavenly messenger
- ___ Father, Mother and children form one

The word on the jumble tower says:

___ ___ ___ ___ ___ ___ ___ ___ ___ ___

(Lehi was very happy to have this kind of record of his ancestors!)

Rebellion

Use the code symbols given to figure out what the rest of the symbols are and find out the meaning of the puzzle.

1 Nephi 7

...in the which rebellion they were desirous to return to the land of Jerusalem...

1 Nephi 7:7

Nephi is Freed!

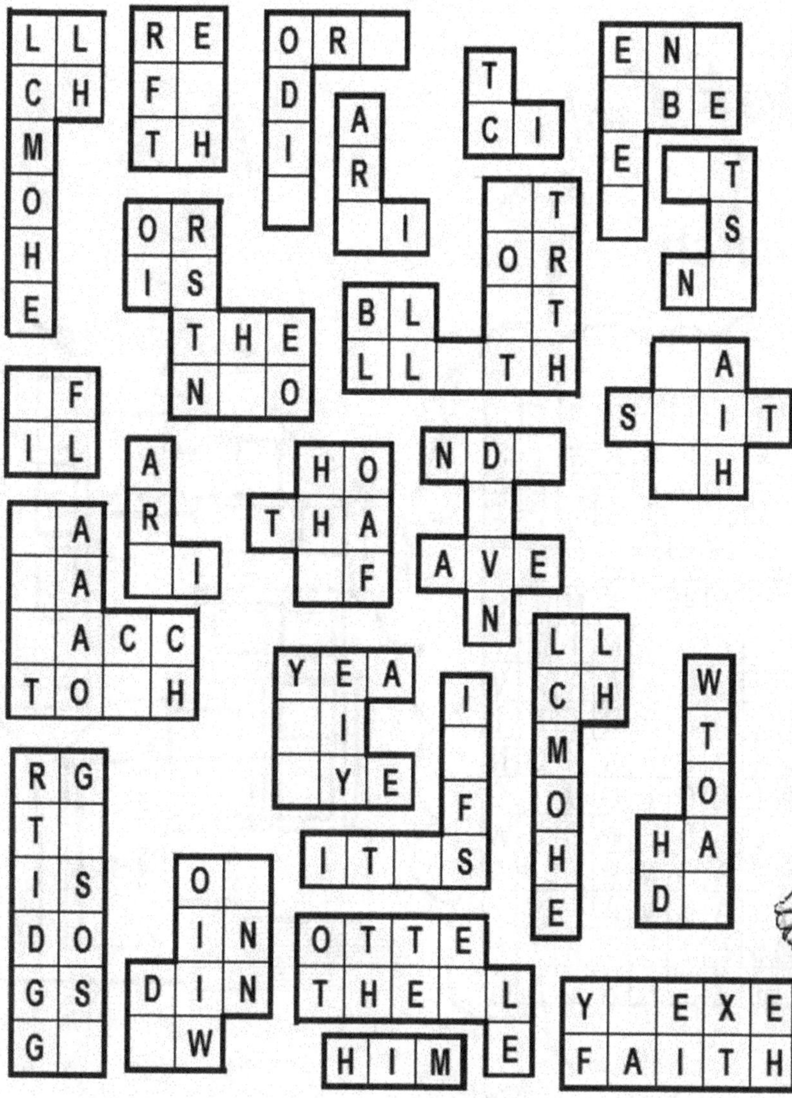

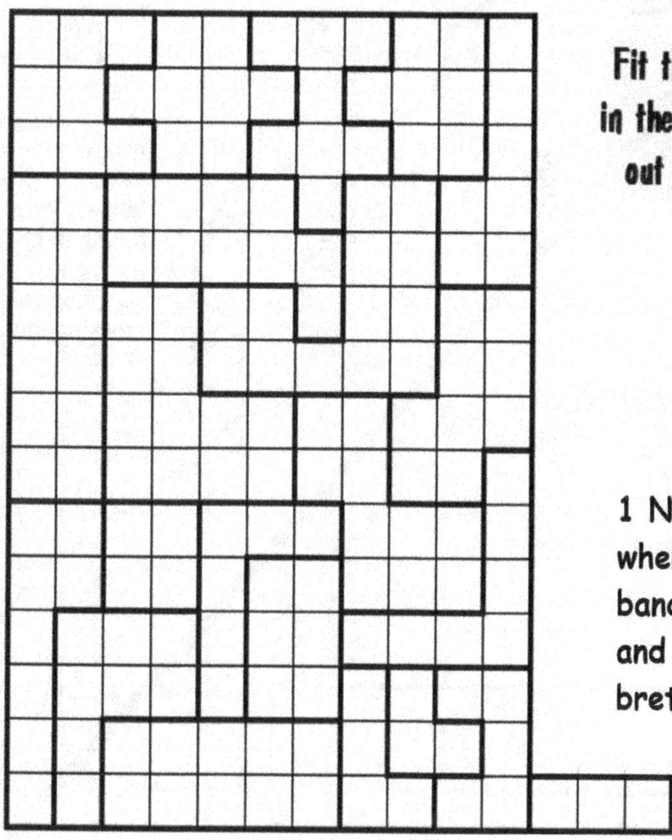

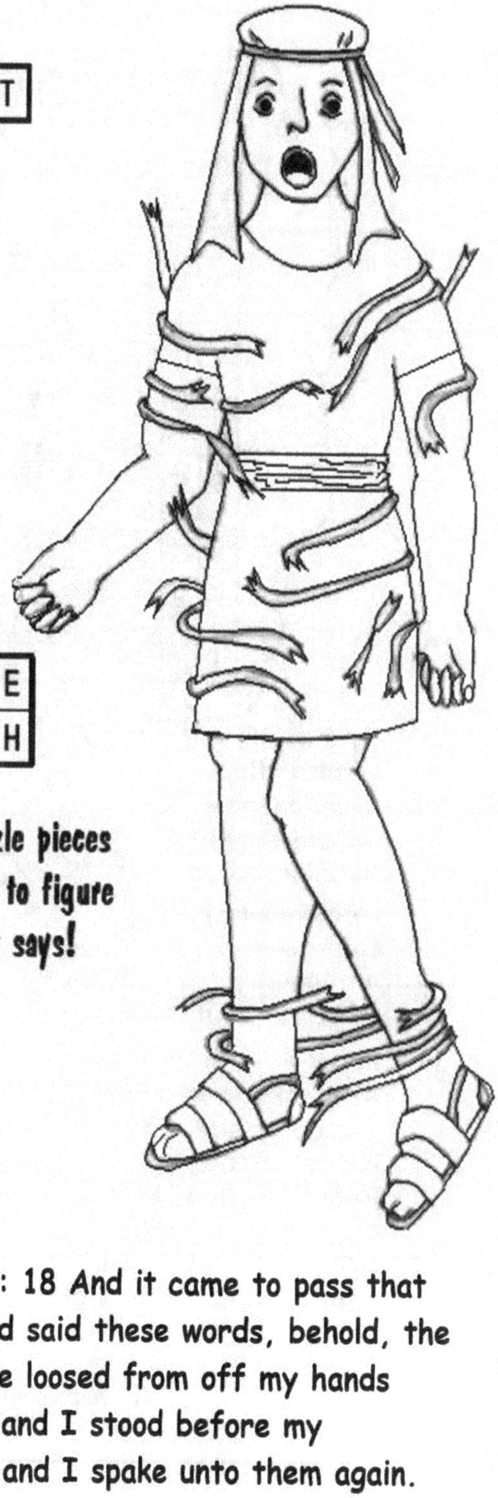

Fit the puzzle pieces in the frame to figure out what it says!

1 Nephi 1: 18 And it came to pass that when I had said these words, behold, the bands were loosed from off my hands and feet, and I stood before my brethren, and I spake unto them again.

The Tree of Life

1 Nephi 8

Wordsearch

Tree of Life

N	R	O	C	S	P	A	C	I	O	U	S	F	L
T	N	E	R	A	P	E	L	A	M	A	N	I	S
M	I	S	T	R	E	E	O	F	L	I	F	E	E
N	E	P	H	I	H	C	V	P	E	O	P	L	E
P	G	D	E	A	G	I	E	L	U	O	S	D	D
A	N	E	I	H	I	O	O	E	T	E	N	T	L
R	I	M	R	J	H	V	F	U	I	N	I	M	I
T	D	A	O	I	O	H	G	M	U	A	A	A	V
A	L	H	N	C	V	Y	O	E	R	R	T	N	I
K	I	S	R	L	K	E	D	L	F	R	N	O	N
E	U	A	O	I	H	I	R	O	I	O	U	I	G
G	B	M	D	N	'	E	N	D	B	W	O	S	W
R	S	L	I	G	H	T	A	G	N	P	F	I	A
E	S	S	E	N	K	R	A	D	V	A	I	V	T
A	M	A	E	R	D	S	F	I	L	T	H	Y	E
T	I	E	D	U	T	I	T	T	A	H	O	N	R

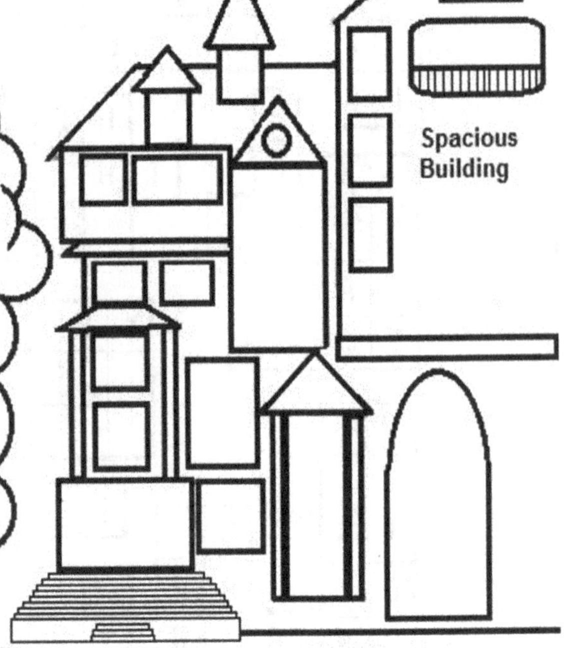

Tree of Life
The Iron Rod
Love of God
Spacious Field
Building River
Mocking Nephi
Darkness Scorn Cling
Ashamed Laman Filthy
Partake Soul Mist Voice
Fountain Hand Lost
Attitude Head Joy
Lemuel Body Sam
Parent Sariah
People Vision Tent
Narrow Fruit High
Dream Great Seed
Light Living Water Path

How to Draw Little People:

River of
Filthy Water

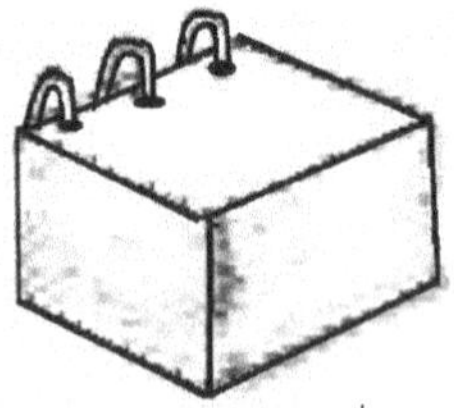

Draw some little people following the path and some people falling away, and falling in the river, and some in the spacious building mocking the others

The remaining letters will form a phrase:

_ _ _ _ _ _   _ _ _ _ _ _ _

Lehi's Vision of the Tree of Life

The fruit which was desirable above all other fruit

Nephi listens..

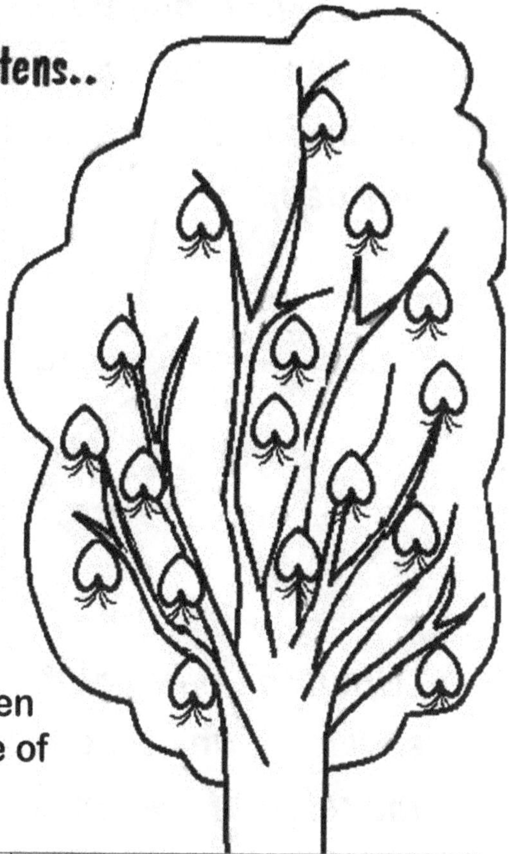

And it came to pass that I beheld others pressing forward, and they came forth and caught hold of the end of the rod of iron; and they did press forward through the mist of darkness, clinging to the rod iron even until they did come forth and partake of the fruit of the tree.

WORD LIST:

Stood
Strait
Partaking
Pressing
Wandered
Ashamed
Desirous
Numberless
Insomuch
Pointing
Beheld
Commenced
Fountain
Spacious
Narrow
Attitude
Lemuel
Laman
Extended
Exceedingly
Darkness
Continually
Writing Air
After Head
River End
Words Led
Multitude
Also Hold
Way By
Rod Had
Fruit Did
Forbidden
Iron High
Lost Unto
Tree Fine

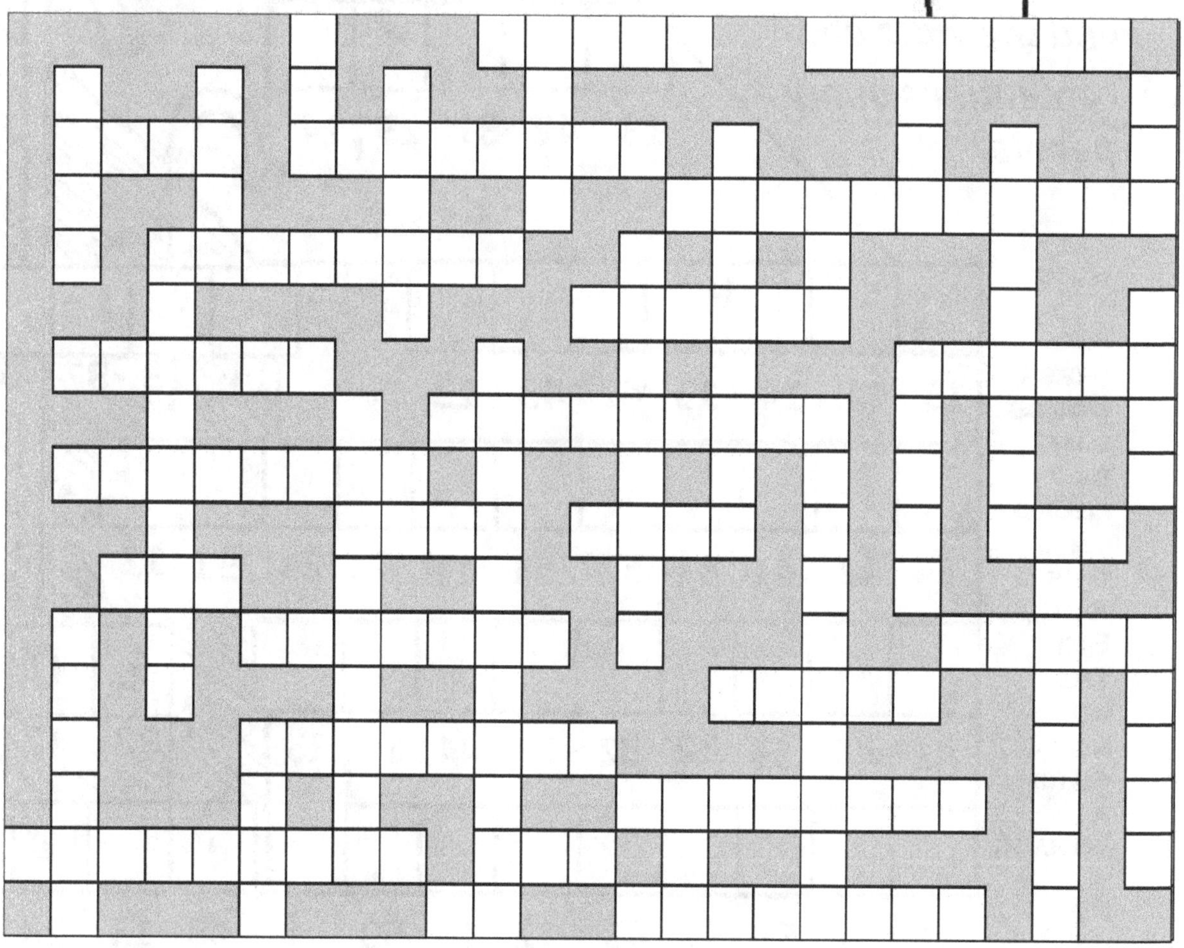

MAKING PLATES

"I have received a commandment of the Lord that I should make these plates, for the special purpose that there should be an account engraven of the ministry of my people" 1 Nephi 9:3-4

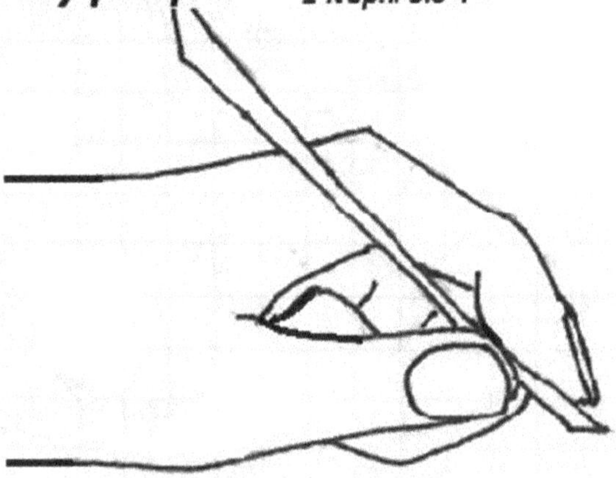

Can you figure out the code?

ONE WORD IS DONE FOR YOU

"Upon the other plates should be an account of the reign of the kings and the wars and contentions of my people"

23 24 22 42 14 12

13 42 31 23 14

NOTE: ALL THESE WORDS CAN BE FOUND ON THIS PAGE, BUT THEY DO NOT MAKE A PHRASE

13 44 14 13 42 43 23

14 23 32 34 51

54 42 41 41 52 51 11 41 23 51 12

41 44 33 12 32 12 44 11 23

L O R D
33 42 14 11

41 32 51 32 43 12 14 53

43 13 23 52 21

LEHI PROPHESIES OF THE MESSIAH

"...a prophet would the Lord God raise up among the Jews...a Messiah..

One long awaited _ _ _ _ _ _ _ ( ) SHEISAMC

One who rescues _ _ _ _ _ _ ( ) ORAVISH

One who buys back _ _ _ _ _ _ _ _ ( ) EMEDERERR

All the people of the earth _ _ _ _ _ _ _ ( ) DIMNAKIN

Those who speak for God _ _ _ _ _ _ _ _ ( ) STREPOPSH

Bear witness or testimony (past tense) _ _ _ _ _ _ _ _ _ ( ) DISTEFETET

The fastener on a shoe (Biblical term) _ _ _ _ _ _ _ ( ) LECITATH

Encouraging others to do good _ _ _ _ _ _ _ _ _ ( ) THEGOIXNRA

A mission or calling to serve _ _ _ _ _ _ _ _ ( ) TRININSMY

When you unscramble these words, there will be one letter left over each time. Put those letters in the spaces below to form a new word.

_ _ _ _ _ _ _ _ _

THE OLIVE TREE

Can you find two leaves that are exactly alike?

1 Nephi 10:12-14

Can you find these hidden items?

Camel
Tent
Brass Plates
Sword
Liahona
Foot
Arrowhead
Bread
Scroll
Trumpet
Honeybee
Fish

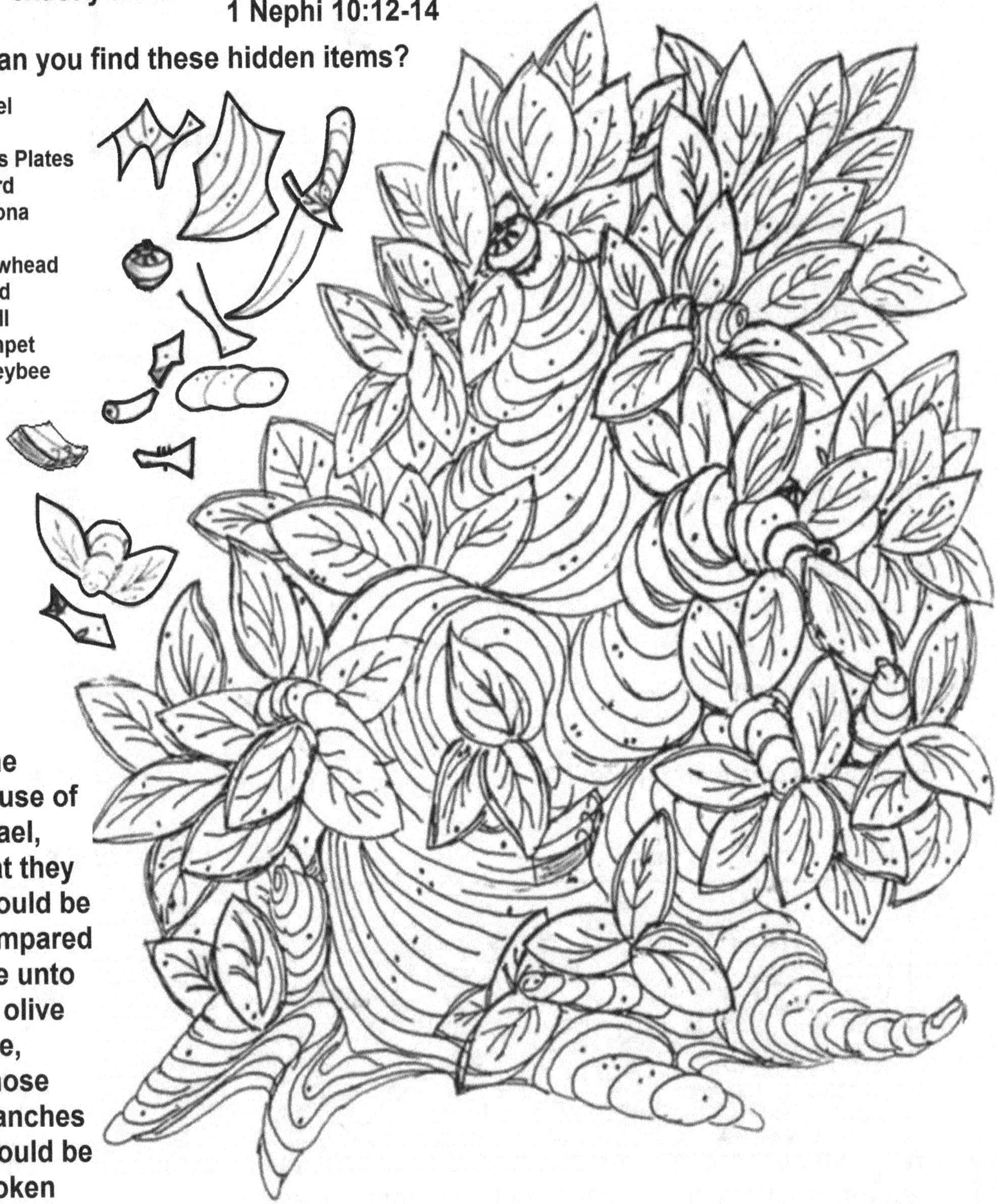

..the House of Israel, that they should be compared like unto an olive tree, whose branches should be broken off...

The Iron Rod

Numberless
Concourses
Forbidden
Darkness
Spacious
Clinging
Extended
Beckoned
Insomuch
Fountain
Forward
Partake
Fingers
Ashamed
Caught
Obtain
Narrow
Tasted Rod
Fruit Air
River God
Many
Speak
Stood
Earth
Above
Iron
Mist
Path
Cast
Tree
Pressing
Come
Eyes
Pass
Great

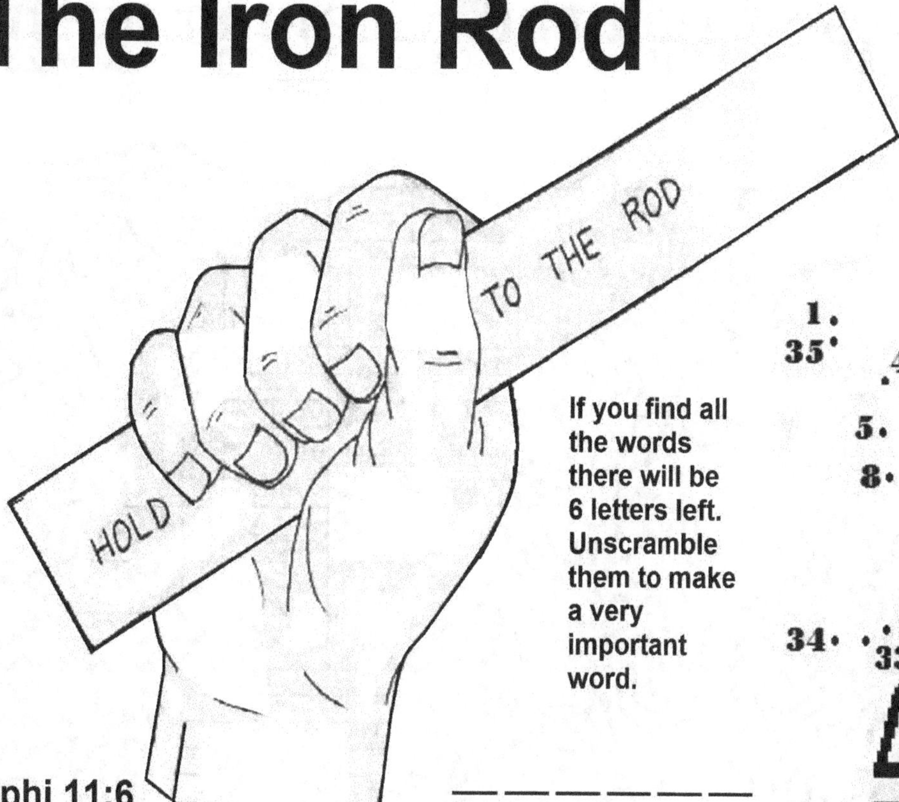

If you find all the words there will be 6 letters left. Unscramble them to make a very important word.

_ _ _ _ _ _

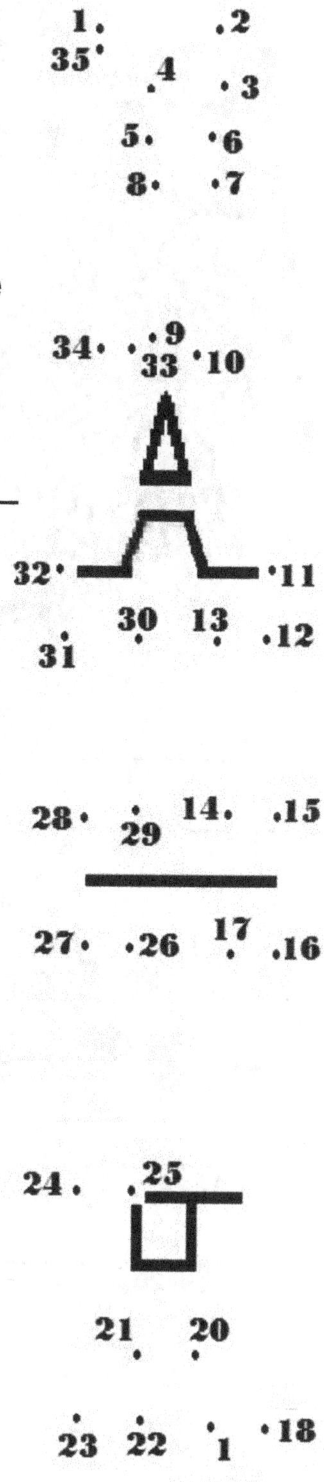

1 Nephi 11:6

And blessed art thou, Nephi, because thou believest in the son of the most high God, wherefore thou shalt behold the things which thou hast desired.

B	E	C	K	O	N	E	D	N	E	V	O	B	A
E	H	G	R	E	A	T	M	I	S	T	F	C	S
M	N	P	A	S	S	H	T	A	P	O	O	F	H
O	A	U	G	H	T	E	S	T	A	N	R	O	A
C	R	T	M	A	N	Y	R	B	C	U	B	U	M
S	R	C	I	B	H	E	S	O	I	D	I	N	E
R	O	D	I	R	E	S	U	T	O	O	D	T	D
E	W	R	I	V	E	R	A	R	U	O	D	A	E
G	O	A	R	N	S	S	L	E	S	T	E	I	K
N	T	W	K	E	T	K	A	E	P	S	N	N	A
I	S	R	S	E	G	N	I	S	S	E	R	P	T
F	A	O	D	R	H	C	U	M	O	S	N	I	R
D	C	F	C	L	I	N	G	I	N	G	O	D	A
E	A	R	T	H	E	X	T	E	N	D	E	D	P

Knowest Thou the Meaning of the Tree?

5 10 15 20 25 30

Use the numbers of the letters from the words in the title to figure out what the words in the blanks below say

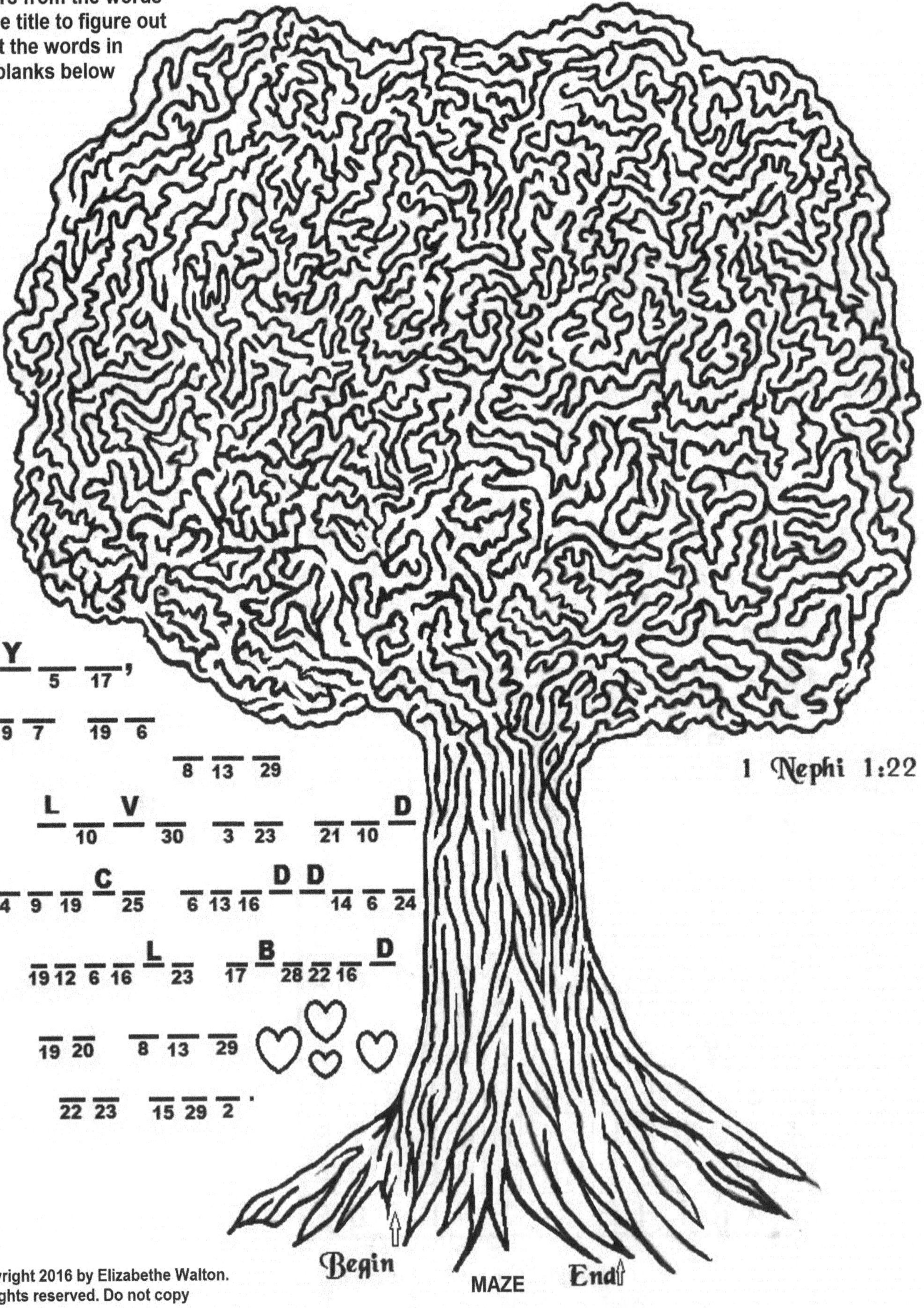

MAZE

1 Nephi 1:22

Y __(5) __(17),

__(19) __(7)   __(19) __(6)

__(8) __(13) __(29)

L __(10) V __(30)   __(3) __(23)   __(21) __(10) D

__(4) __(9) __(19) C __(25)   __(6) __(13) __(16) D D __(14) __(6) __(24)

__(19) __(12) __(6) __(16) L __(23)   __(17) B __(28) __(22) __(16) D

__(19) __(20)   __(8) __(13) __(29)

__(22) __(23)   __(15) __(29) __(2).

The Good Shepherd

1 Nephi 13:41
...and the words of the Lamb shall be made known in the records of thy seed, as well as in the records of the twelve apostles of the Lamb; wherefore they both shall be established in one; for there is one God and one Shepherd over all the earth.

How to draw a sheep

Now draw your own sheep below

A D E F G H I L N O
L N O P R S T V

Use the code above to decode the message below

1 Nephi 13:41

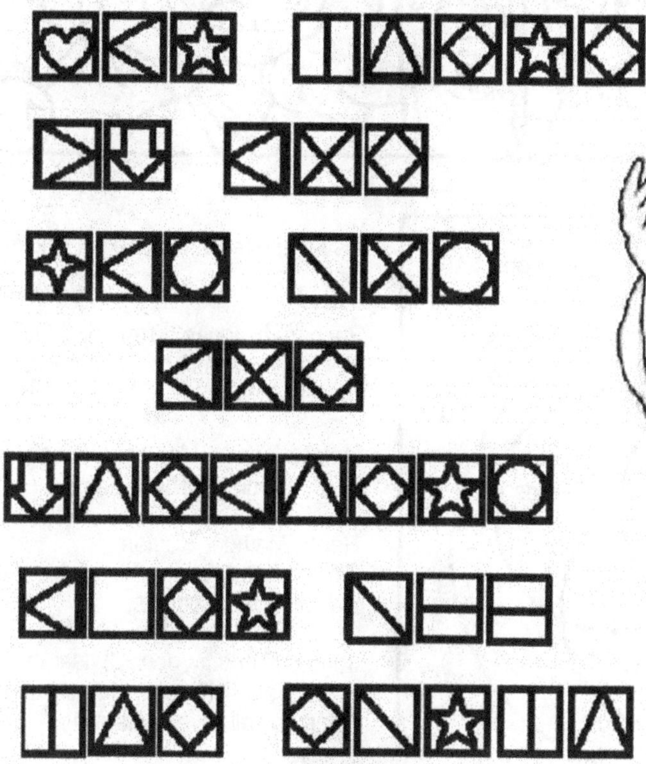

Twelve Nephite Disciples

3 Nephi 19:4 is where all the names are listed

Can you figure out which one is which?

You can use the circles below to help you figure things out!

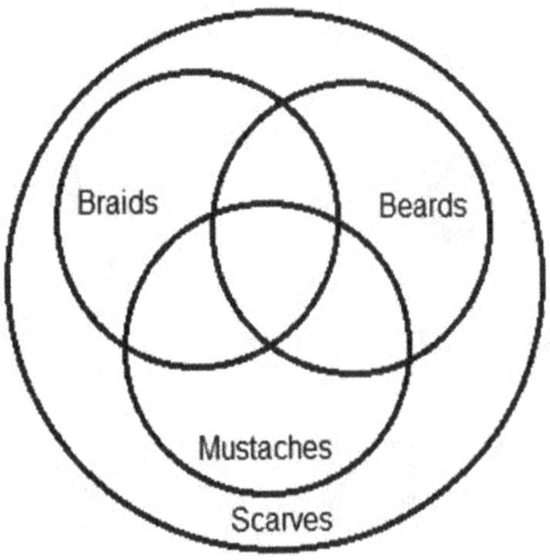

Use these facts to figure out who is who!

Zechariah, Jonas2, Timothy, Mathoni, Nephi, Jeremiah and Shemnon all have braids.

Isaiah, Jonas1, Mathoni, Jonas2, and Jeremiah all have beards.

Nephi, Mathoni, Kumen, Timothy, and Kumenonhi all are wearing head scarves.

Jonas1, Timothy, Jonas2, Isaiah, Mathoniahah, Kumen, Mathoni and Shemnon all have mustaches.

Who is Who?

1. ______________
2. ______________
3. ______________
4. ______________
5. ______________
6. ______________
7. ______________
8. ______________
9. ______________
10. ______________
11. ______________
12. ______________

THE GREAT DIVIDE

V E I L E D — Modest women in biblical times were ___________.

_ _ _ _ _ — One name for Satan: he is a _______________.

_ _ _ _ — Satan desires that all men should be _______ like him.

_ _ _ — Satan wants us to ______, steal, kill and do evil things.

_ _ _ _ _ _ — More than one of the thing below

_ _ _ _ _ — A large number of "Deseret" or honeybees

_ _ _ _ — Battles or conflicts between many people

_ _ _ — Past form of the verb "is"

G R E A S Y — Oily or fatty things are ____________

Y E A R S — Multiple sets of 12 months

_ _ _ _ — Simple or not difficult

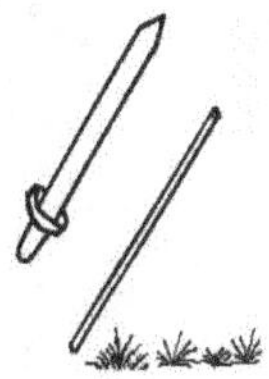

_ _ _ — A way of saying "Yes" in bible language

_ _ _ _ _ _ — To sleep very lightly, or to feel very tired

_ _ _ _ _ — A weapon like a long knife

_ _ _ _ — Long thin poles or sticks (also the Word of God in iron)

_ _ _ — Grass rolls to make an "instant" lawn

In the puzzle above, each succeeding word is an anagram (a word with the same letters but arranged differently) of the previous word, less one letter.

There are several sets. One word is done for you.

And He Went Forth Upon the Many Waters

Word List:

Promised
white
came
Tree
against
wrought
church
land
Nephi
land
before
saw
humble
Gentiles
people
people
prosper
unto
the
out

After the vision of the abominable ______
and ______ vision of the
______ of Life
______
______ that
the ______
came ______ of captivity
and these ______
were ______ and fair
like unto his own ______
______ they were slain.

And they ______ forth
and did ______
in the ______
The Spirit ______ upon them
to come to the ______ land
because they were ______
The wrath of God was ______ all those
who fought ______ them.

1 Nephi 13: 1-17

You can find my name by filling the words in above

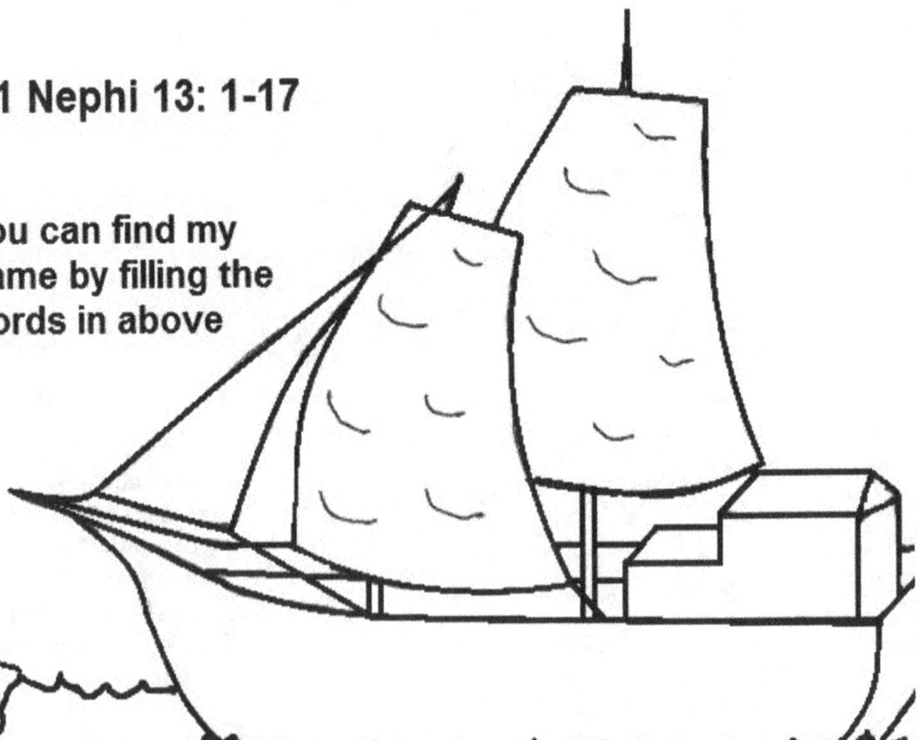

A RECORD OF THE JEWS VIA THE GENTILES

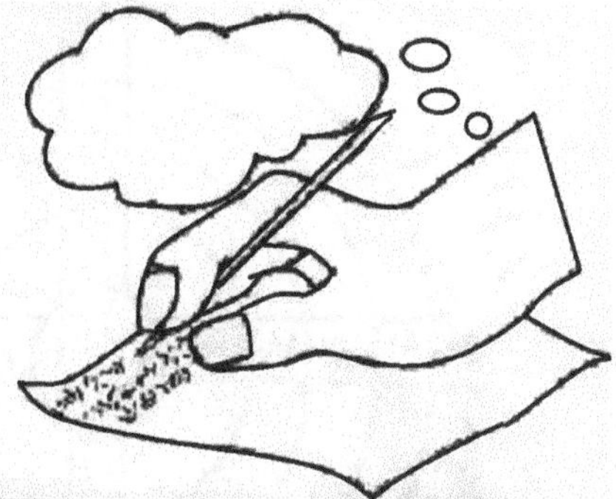

1 Nephi 13: 23

Behold, it proceedeth out of the mouth of a Jew.

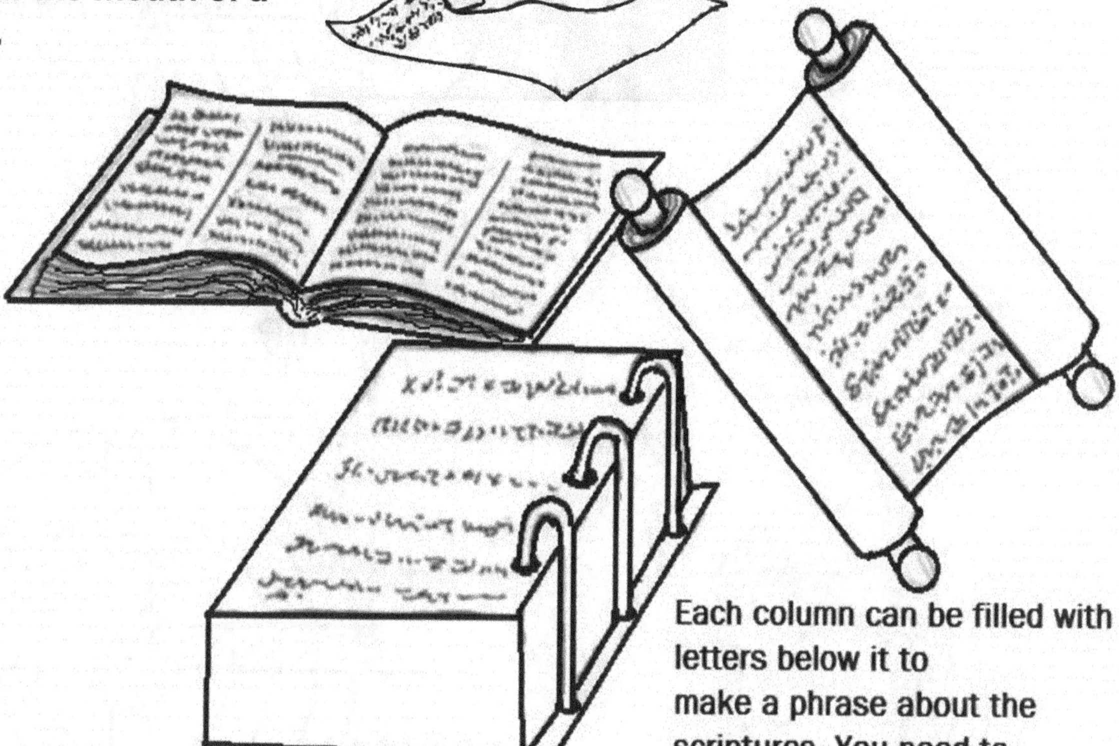

Each column can be filled with letters below it to make a phrase about the scriptures. You need to figure out which letter goes where:

Wordfall

T	H	K	N	N	S	A	W	N	Y	C	F	D	H	M	V	T	C	B	O	U	N
T	A	E	E	P	L	A	I	A	I	A	N	R	O	A	R	E	H	E	M	E	S
T	H	I		G			W	H			H			P		E		I	E		

These Things Shall Come Forth Unto Thy Seed

In your mind, turn each ring of the wheel until they line up in such a manner as to form five letter words. The words read from the outside in.

An

A ___ ___ ___ ___

S ___ A ___ ___

with

A ___ ___ ___ ___

P ___ ___ ___ ___

1 Nephi 13:35

to

B ___ ___ ___ ___

F ___ ___ ___ ___

P ___ ___ ___ ___

T ___ ___ T ___

Make up your own code!

For There Shall Be One Shepherd Over All the Earth

A	
B	
C	
D	
E	
F	
G	
H	
I	
J	
K	
L	
M	
N	
O	
P	
Q	
R	
S	
T	
U	
V	
W	
X	
Y	
Z	

⊙ N ♉   T ♏ ♌   T ♐ □ ♌

♊ B □ ♌ T ♏   T ♏ ♈ T

♅ ♌   S ♏ ♈ ♓ ♓

□ ♈ N ♐ ♍ ♌ S T

♏ ♐ □ S ♌ ♓ ♍   □ N T B

♈ ♓ ♓

N ♈ T ♐ B N S

1 Nephi 13:41

The vowels are:

♈	♌	♐	B	□
a	e	i	o	u

Some consonants are:

T	□	S	♏
t	m	s	h

Can you figure out the rest of the symbols and find out what the phrase says?

See 1 Nephi 13:42 if you need help.

Write something below in your own code!

There are Save Two Churches Only

Fill in the missing vowels to find out what the scripture says:

F__r th__ t__m__ c__m__th s__ __th th__ L__mb __f G__d

th__t __ w__ll w__rk __ gr__ __t __nd __ m__rv__l__ __s

w__rk __m__ng th__ ch__ldr__n __f m__n: __ w__rk

wh__ch sh__ll b__ __v__rl__st__ng, __ __th__r __n th__

__n__ h__nd __r th__ __th__r – __ __th__r t__ th__

c__nv__nc__ng __f th__m __nt__ p__ __c__ __nd l__f__

__t__rn__l, __r __nt__ th__ d__l__v__r__nc__ __f th__m t__

th__ h__rdn__ss __f th__ __r h__ __rts __nd th__

bl__ndn__ss __f th__ __r m__nds __nt__ th__ __r b__ __ng

br__ __ght d__wn __nt__ c__pt__v__ty, __nd __lso __nt__

d__str__ct__ __n, b__th t__mp__r__lly __nd sp__r__t__ __lly

__cc__rd__ng t__ th__ c__pt__v__ty __f th__ d__v__l.

1 Nephi 14:7

He Shall Write Concerning the End of the World

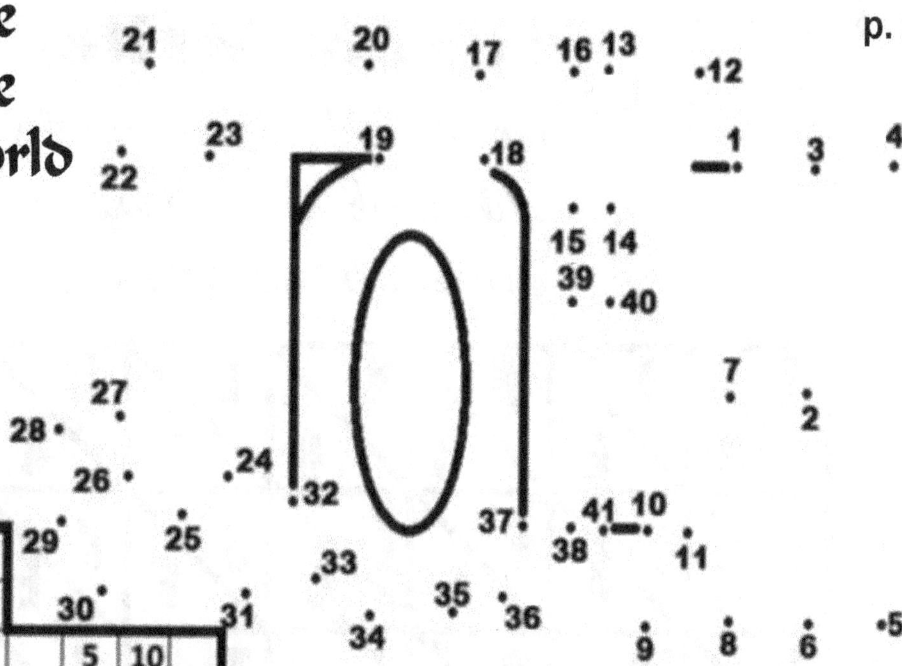

Find out what the message says by using the table below. Each number is the total of two numbers on the grid.

4	7	10	6	9	12				
6	8	7		6	3		5	10	
									E
5	8	7	9	8	7				
11	4	6	8	5	9	7	8		
6	3		5	10	7				
9	11	1	4						

1 Nephi 14:20

	1	2	3	4	5	6
1	M	F	B	T	O	E
2	F	P	T	O	E	S
3	B	T	O	E	S	L
4	T	O	E	V	L	H
5	O	E	W	L	H	A
6	E	N	L	H	A	D

So if the puzzle has 6, then it could be 1+5 or 2+4 or 3+3. If you look on the grid, each of those combinations is the letter O, so a 6 means O. But be careful, sometimes there is more than one letter possible....

He Shall Write

Behold, one of the twelve apostles
of the Lamb, who shall write
concerning the end of the world

B / R	A / E	H / C	K / O	L / T	D / K	I / H	Y / E	P / S
I / H	F / A	E / L	L / D	S / F	K / E	Y / E	O / A	U / N
D / B	W / T	R / M	E / I	T / S	I / E	M / S	S / A	O / N
I / Y	T / S	H / P	Y / I	N / U	A / G	S / F	W / P	O / H
E / I	C / W	H / P	H / M	K / A	E / V	G / E	A / B	Y / E
							O / E	N / U

Cross out all the vowels that are on the top half
Cross out all these letters F J K P Q U
Cross out all the B C D M R T W that are on the bottom
except B in row 5

Cross out S on the bottom
except on row 1
and all S on row 3

Cross out GVY
on the top half

The remaining letters
have a message

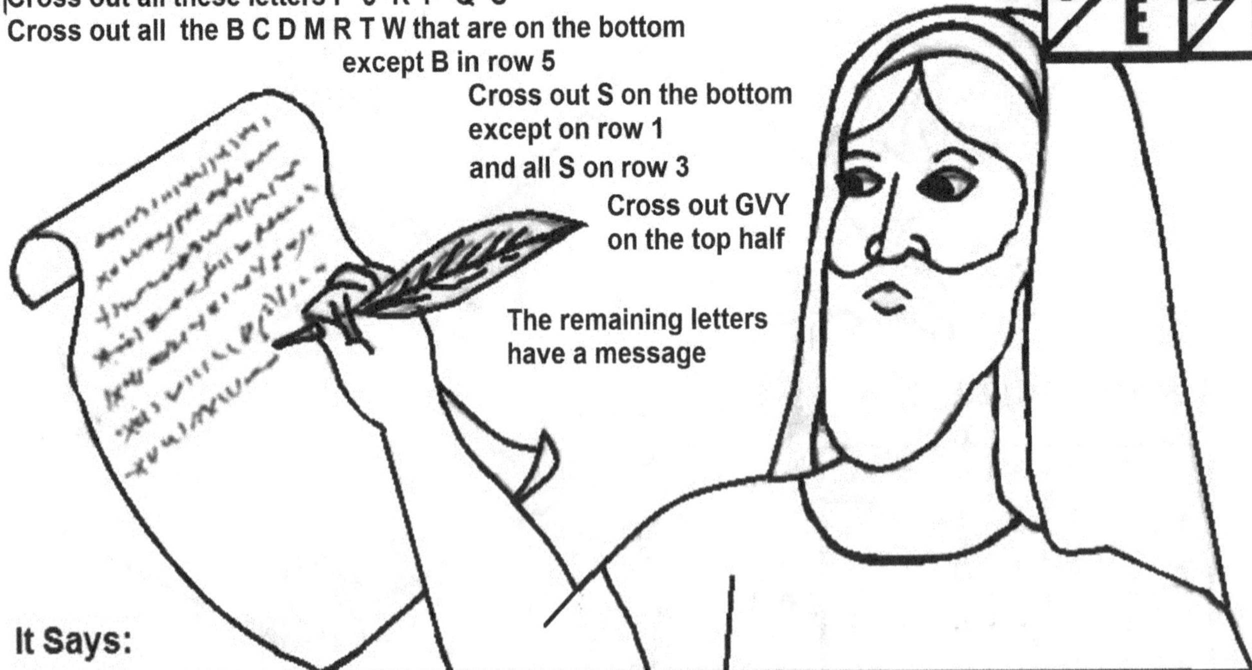

It Says:

Nephi Prays for Knowledge

You can figure out the missing words by reading 1 Nephi 15:1-8 The letters in the boxes will fill in the word at the end.

Because of the
___ ___ ___ [ ] ___ ___ ___ ___ ___
of their hearts, when Nephi's brothers
___ [ ] ___ ___ ___ ___ ___ ___ of
the teachings, they did not
___ ___ ___ ___ ___ ___ ___ [ ] ___ ___ ___ ___ ___ .
Unlike his
___ ___ ___ [ ] ___ ___ ___ ___ ___ ,
Nephi was
___ ___ ___ [ ] ___ ___ ___ ___ ___
by grief
___ ___ ___ ___ ___ [ ] ___ ___
of what he had seen in vision
___ ___ ___ [ ] ___ ___ ___ ___ ___ ___ ___ ___ ___ ___
his seed. His brothers
___ ___ ___ ___ ___ ___ ___ [ ] ___ ___ ___
among themselves.
Nephi asked them, "Have ye
___ ___ ___ ___ ___ [ ] ___ ___ ___ ___
of the Lord?
Then he explained how Lehi had
___ ___ ___ [ ] ___ ___ ___ ___
of the Jews (the olive tree) as the
[ ] ___ ___ ___ ___ ___ ___ ___ ___ ___
branches and the Gentiles
as those who were grafted in.
But Nephi was still sorrowful because
he had foreseen the
___ ___ ___ ___ ___ ___ ___ ___ ___ ___ ___ ___ ___ ___ ___ ___
of all his seed (descendants.)

1 Nephi 14:5

"It came to pass that I was overcome because of my afflictions ... because of the destruction of my people, for I had beheld their fall."

A Branch of Israel

L1	L5	R3	R1	L1	R3	L8	R1	L1	R7			
R2	R5	L5	R3	L6	L9	R8	L0	R5	R9	R5		
L1	L5	R0	L2	R6	R9	L5	R3	L5	L1	R6		
L0	L5	R3	L2	L2	R5	L1	R4	R5	L7	L5	R3	
L3	R7	R3	R7	R8	R4	R5	L3	R8	R9	L5	R4	L9

Place your pencil tip on the starting letter. From there go right (clockwise) or left (counter-clockwise) as directed by the puzzle to find out what it says.

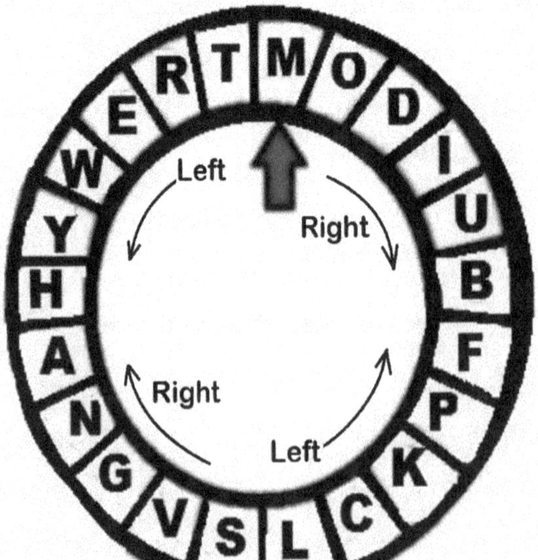

1 Nephi 15: 12

...behold, are we not broken off from the House of Israel, and are we not a branch of the House of Israel?

Nephi's Brothers Ask Him About the Tree of Life

1 Nephi 15:21

"What meaneth this thing?"

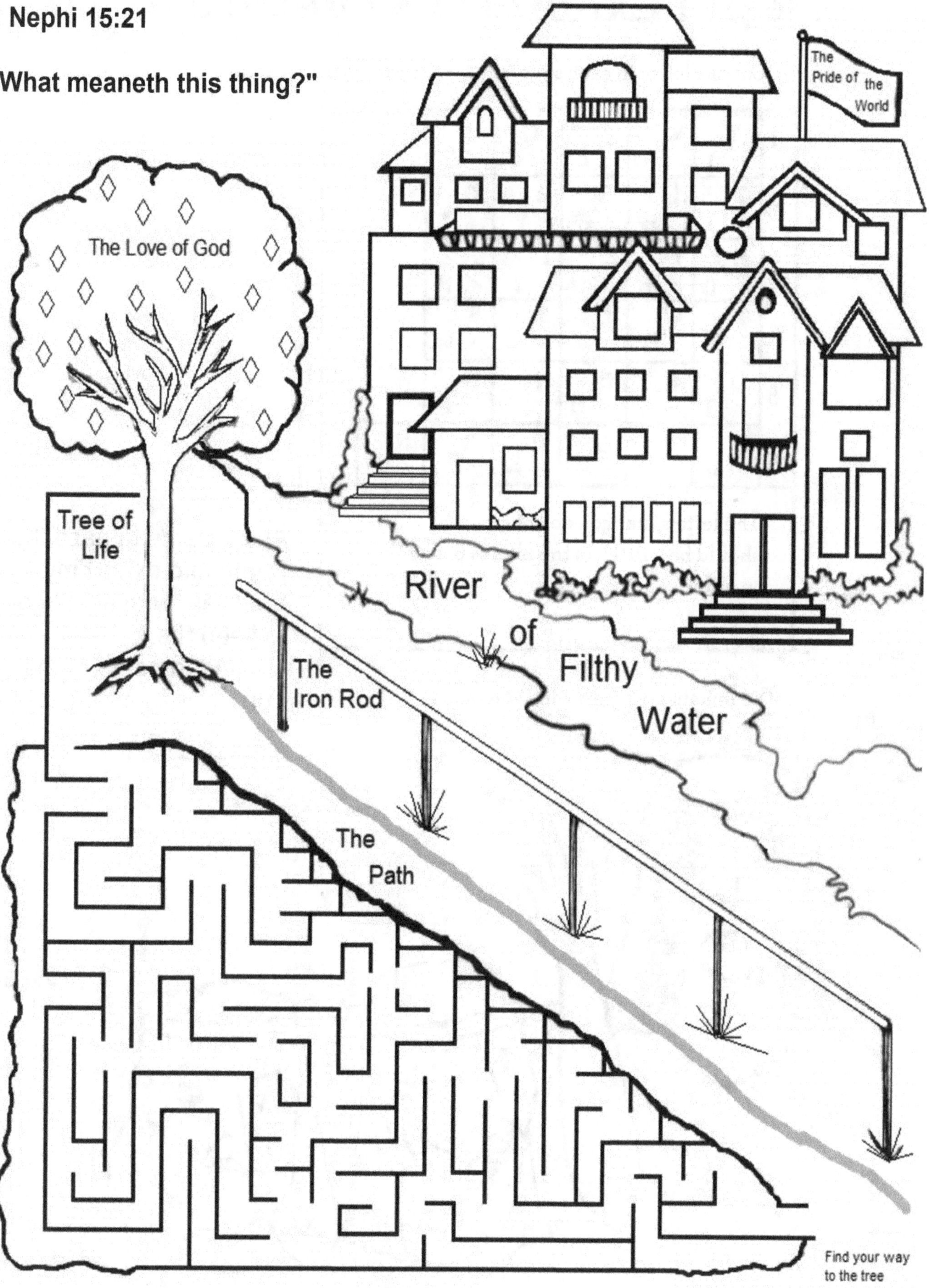

Nephi Exhorts His Brethren

Cross out one letter in each square to form a word reading across.

1	T / A	W / H	F / E	G / U	U / L	
2	G / I	L / R	T / E	A / Y	T / T	
3	A / D	E / K	E / U	T / I	L / H	
4	T / D	W / H	E / E	T / L	R / L	
5	U / T	R / T	H / U	T / T	H / O	
6	S / B	E / P	O / H	A / K	R / E	N / D

The letters that you do not cross out should be written in the blanks below in order:

1. _ _ _ _ _
2. _ _ _ _ _
3. _ _ _ _ _
4. _ _ _ _ _
5. _ _ _ _ _
6. _ _ _ _ _ _

And it came to pass that I, Nephi, did exhort my brethren, with all diligence, to keep the commandments of the Lord.

The remaining letters will then say:

_ _ _   _ _ _ _ _ _ _

_ _ _ _ _ _ _   _ _ _

_ _ _ _ _   _ _   _ _

_ _ _ _

I Nephi 16:2

The Liahona Is Found

Can you figure out where the two spindles should go?

And can you draw them in?

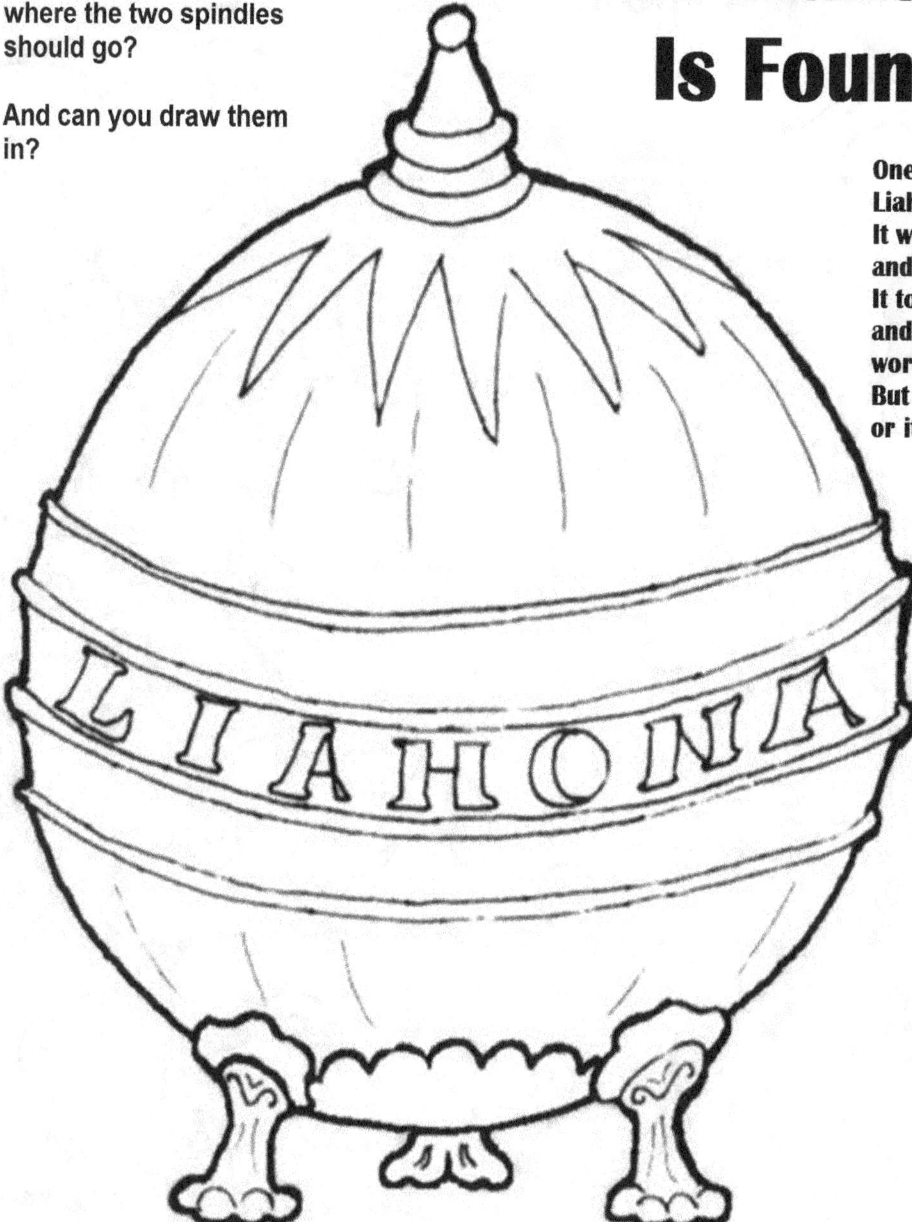

One morning they found the Liahona outside their tent. It was in the shape of a ball and it had spindles on it. It told them which way to go and sometimes it had words written on it. But they had to be obedient or it would not work.

1 Nephi 16:10

"a round ball of curious workmanship, and it was of fine brass. And within the ball were two spindles, and the one pointed the way we should go inot the wilderness."

Start

Find your way to the Liahona:

Help Nephi find four animals for food

FINDING GAME

Now that Nephi has a bow, he asks his father where he should go to find food.

There are animals that Nephi cannot get to. Can you find them?

Camel Travel

Lehi and his family traveled in the wilderness with tents and camels for a long time. Do you know how long?

1 Nephi 17: 4

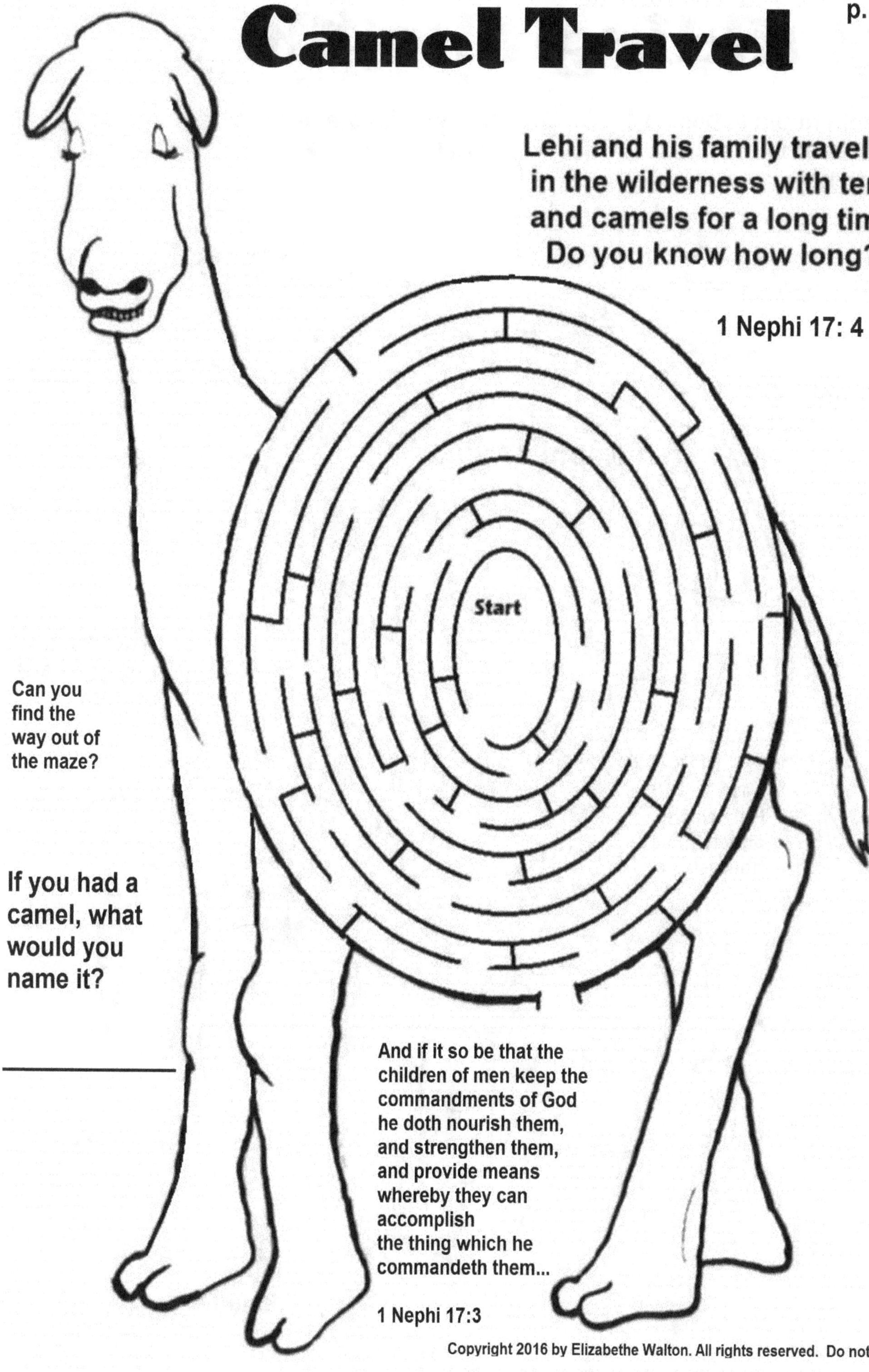

Can you find the way out of the maze?

If you had a camel, what would you name it?

____

And if it so be that the children of men keep the commandments of God he doth nourish them, and strengthen them, and provide means whereby they can accomplish the thing which he commandeth them...

1 Nephi 17:3

Building the Ship

God told Nephi to build a ship. His brothers did not want to help.

Can you do the dot-to-dot to help out?

1 Nephi 17:8

Thou shalt construct a ship, after the manner which I shall show thee...

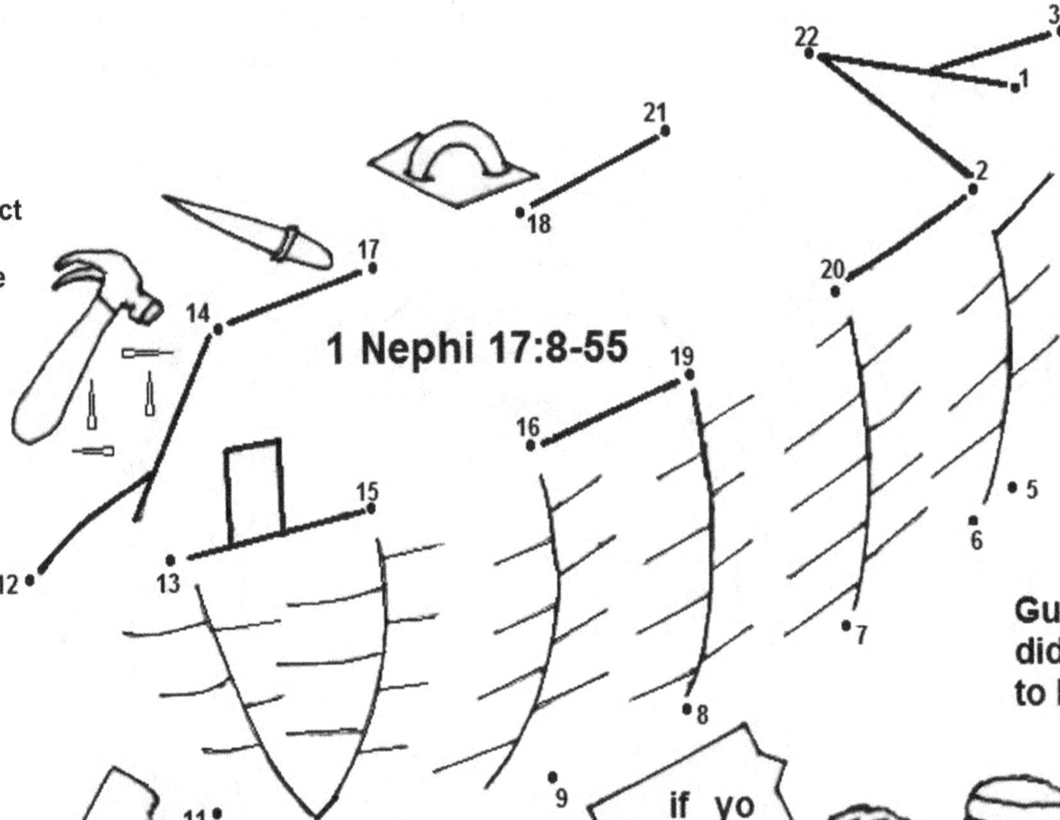

Guess who did not want to help?

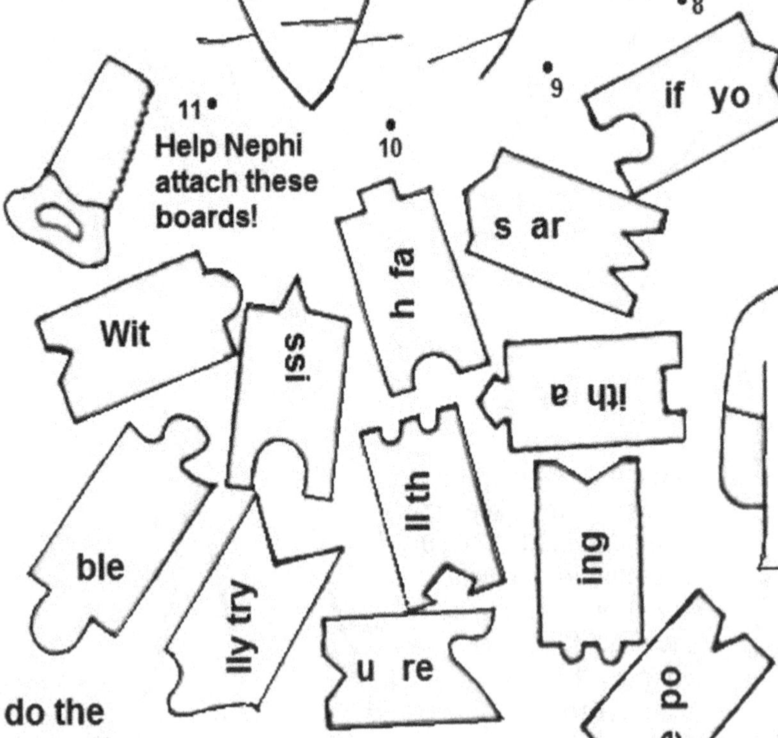

_ _ _ _ _ _ and

_ _ _ _ _ _ _

What do the boards say?

timbers of curious workmanship

NEPHI'S BROTHERS WERE VERY RUDE TO HIM!

1 Nephi 17:23

Nephi answered them:

Do ye believe that our
fathers would have
been led away out
of the hands of the
Egyptians if they had
not hearkened to the
words of the Lord?

You can figure out what the brothers are saying to Nephi by using the code above:

God's Lovely Creation

Put the puzzle pieces together to see what it says. The three dots ... mean the space between words.

1 Nephi 17:36

ey...	...po	ss...	uld
th...	...be	ord	...th
e...L	e...h	t...i	ate
hab	cre	d;...	...th
eat	ho	Beh	th...
old,	d...h	d...t	ed...
ath	he...	...ch	...ha
at...	ear	...in	ren
t...s	...cr	tha	uld
...an	his	ild	ite
th...	...it.	sho	sse

Touch Me Not!

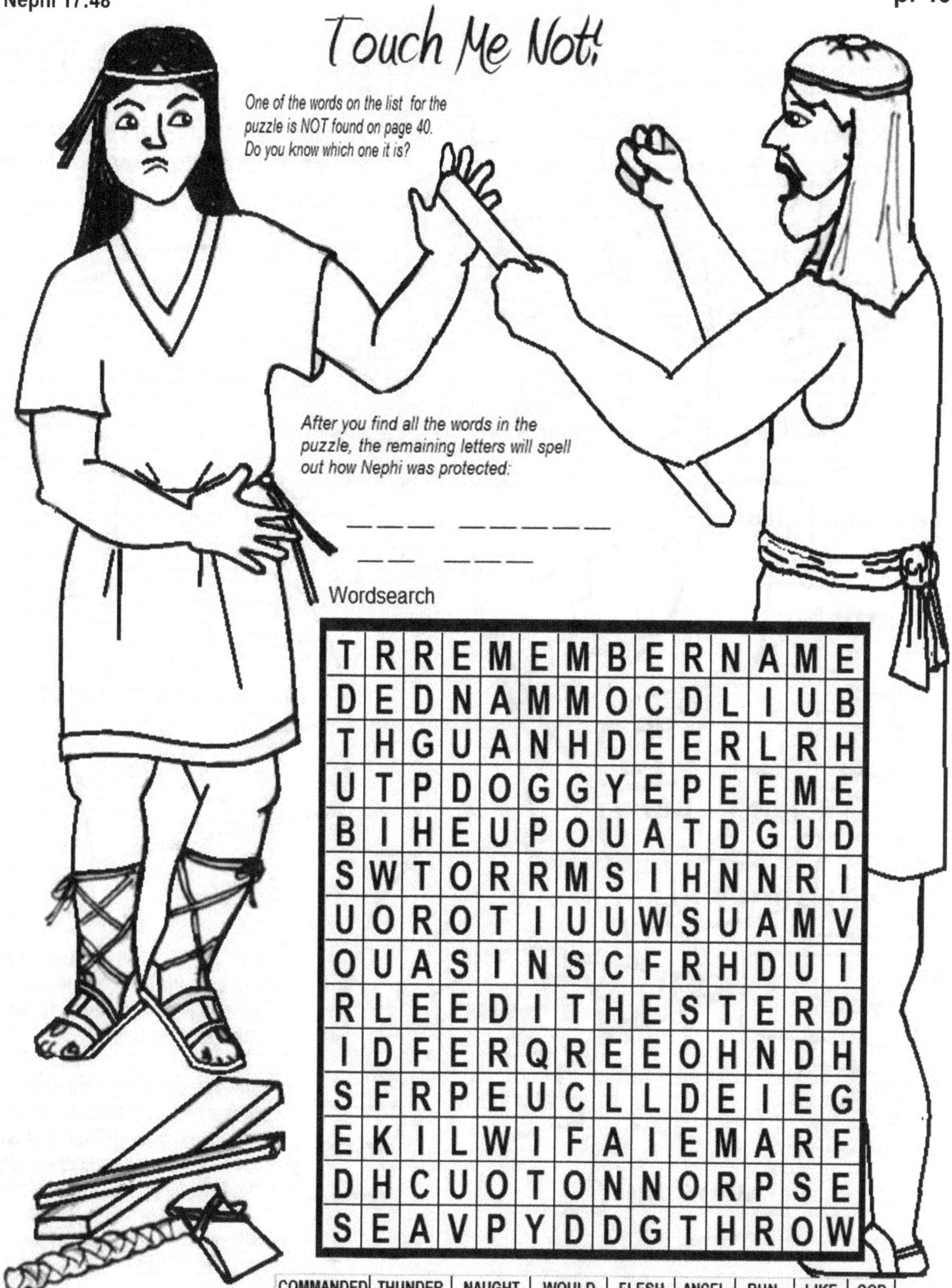

One of the words on the list for the puzzle is NOT found on page 40. Do you know which one it is?

After you find all the words in the puzzle, the remaining letters will spell out how Nephi was protected:

_ _ _ _ _ _ _ _ _ _ _

_ _ _ _ _ _

Wordsearch

T	R	R	E	M	E	M	B	E	R	N	A	M	E
D	E	D	N	A	M	M	O	C	D	L	I	U	B
T	H	G	U	A	N	H	D	E	E	R	L	R	H
U	T	P	D	O	G	G	Y	E	P	E	E	M	E
B	I	H	E	U	P	O	U	A	T	D	G	U	D
S	W	T	O	R	R	M	S	I	H	N	N	R	I
U	O	R	O	T	I	U	U	W	S	U	A	M	V
O	U	A	S	I	N	S	C	F	R	H	D	U	I
R	L	E	E	D	I	T	H	E	S	T	E	R	D
I	D	F	E	R	Q	R	E	E	O	H	N	D	H
S	F	R	P	E	U	C	L	L	D	E	I	E	G
E	K	I	L	W	I	F	A	I	E	M	A	R	F
D	H	C	U	O	T	O	N	N	O	R	P	S	E
S	E	A	V	P	Y	D	D	G	T	H	R	O	W

Wordlist:

COMMANDED	THUNDER	NAUGHT	WOULD	FLESH	ANGEL	RUN	LIKE	GOD
REMEMBER	ASUNDER	WITHER	PAINED	TOUCH	HEART	NAME	SHIP	NOT
DESTROYED	ANGUISH	DEPTHS	FEELING	POWER	FRAME	FEAR	MUST	SEA
DESIROUS	PERISHED	DIVIDE	ROUGH	VOICE	BUILD	LAND	SUCH	FEW
INIQUITY	MURDERS	MURMUR	THROW	EARTH	REED	THEM	BUT	SIN

Nephi Builds a Ship

Put each board of the ship into the right place to see what the message says:

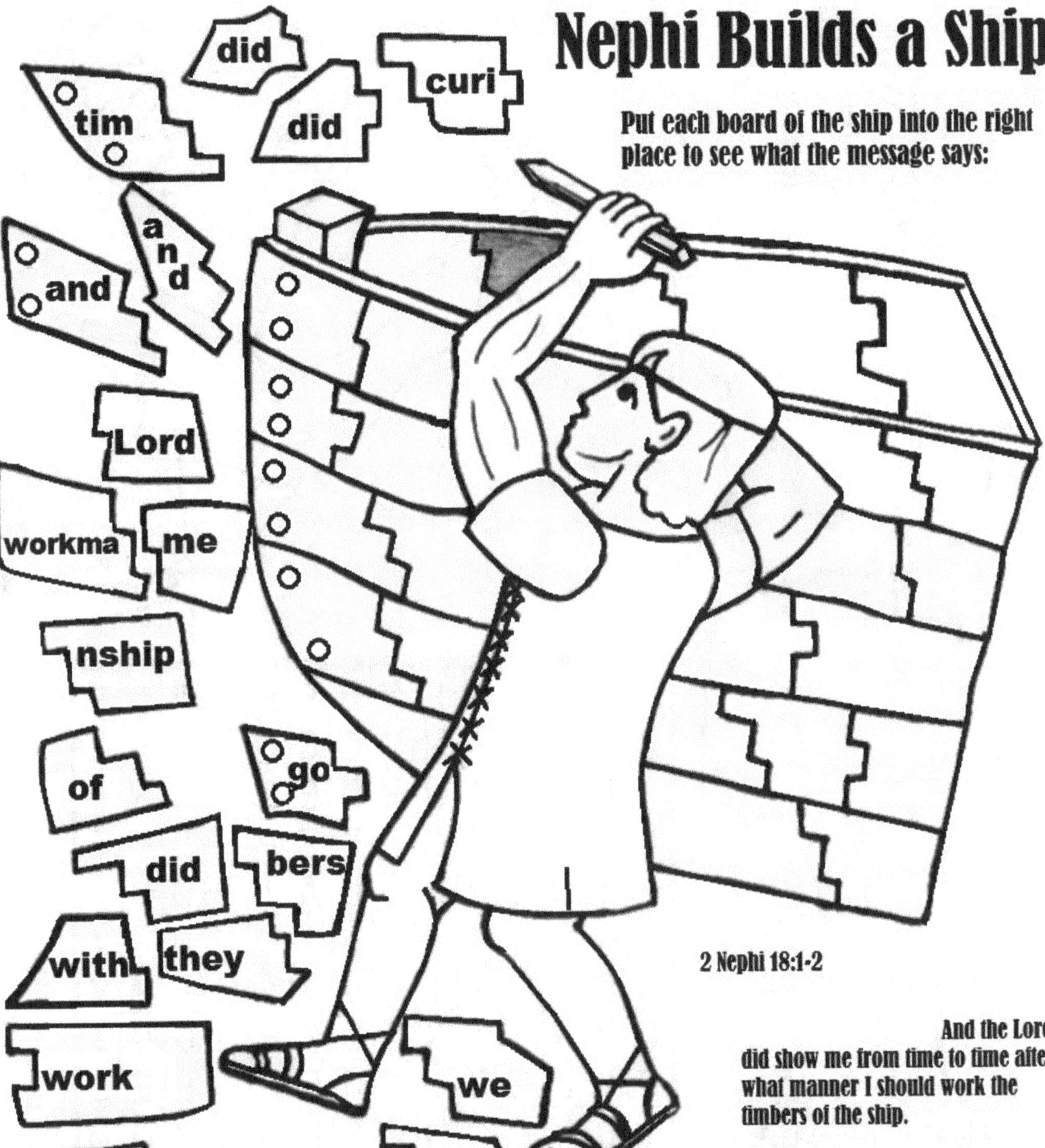

2 Nephi 18:1-2

And the Lord did show me from time to time after what manner I should work the timbers of the ship.

Now I, Nephi, did not work the timbers after the manner which was learned by men, neither did I build the ship after the manner of men; but I did build it after the manner which the Lord had shown unto me; wherefore, it was not after the manner of men.

Sailing to the Promised Land

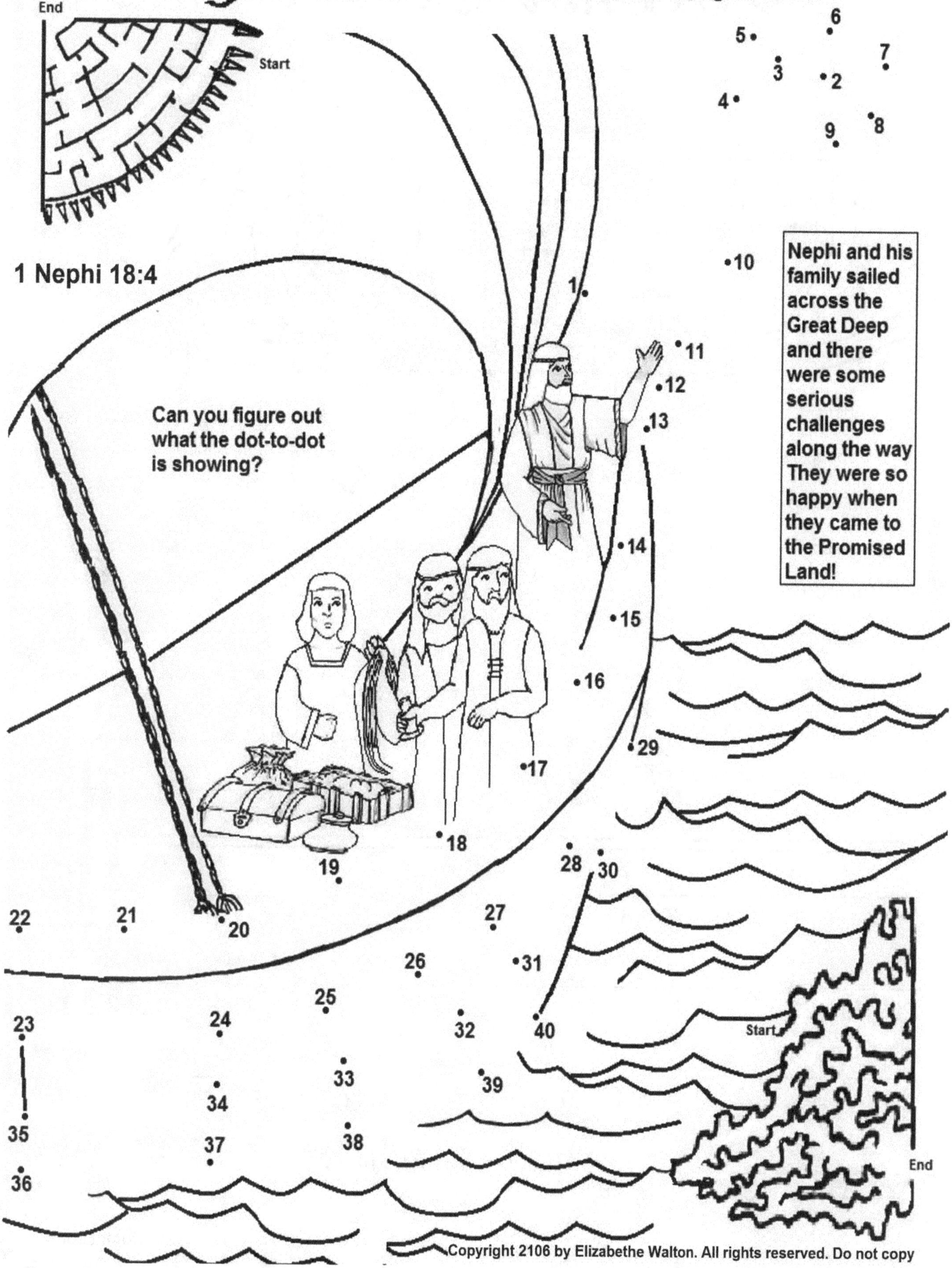

1 Nephi 18:4

Can you figure out what the dot-to-dot is showing?

Nephi and his family sailed across the Great Deep and there were some serious challenges along the way They were so happy when they came to the Promised Land!

A Bad Storm

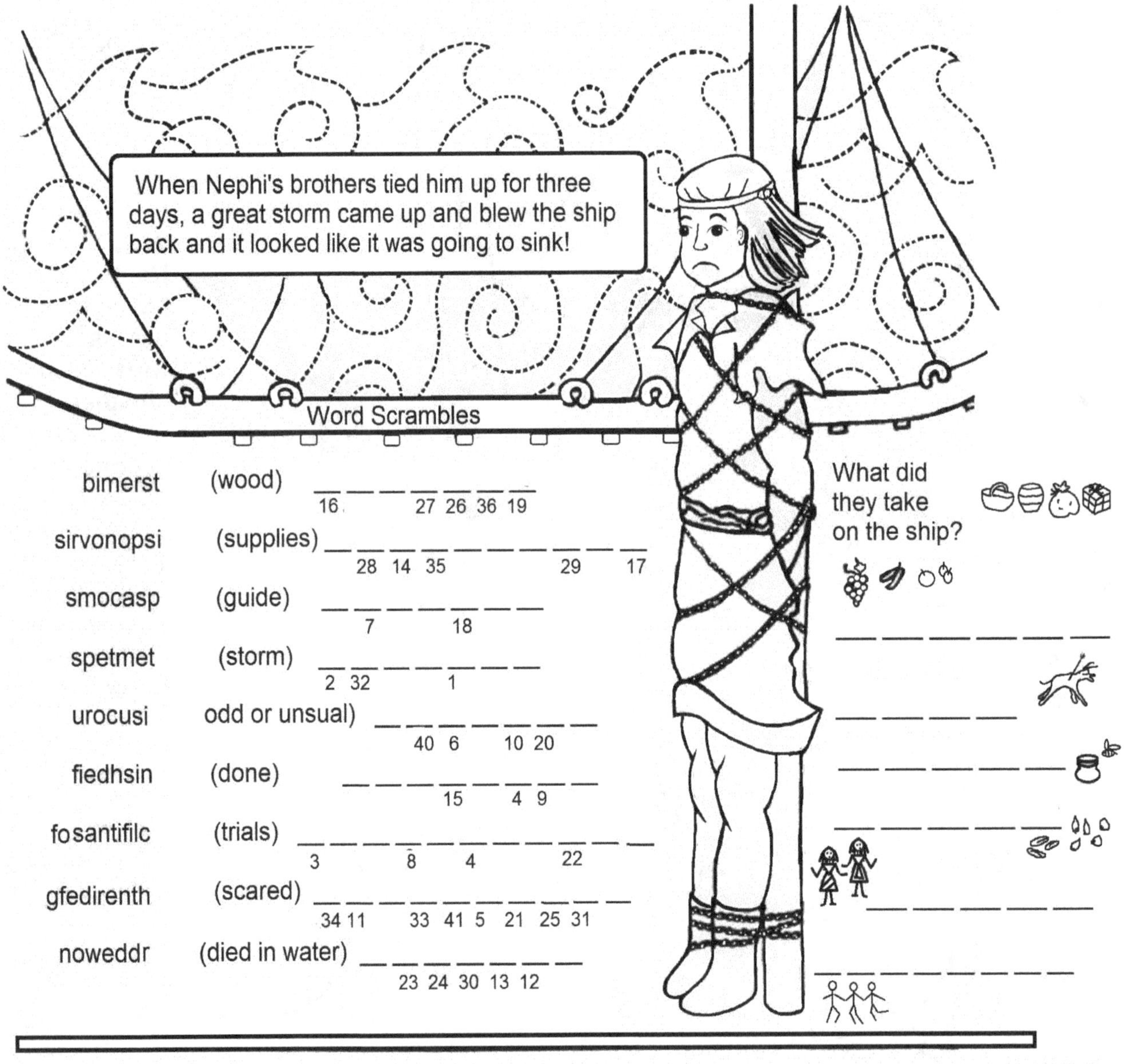

When Nephi's brothers tied him up for three days, a great storm came up and blew the ship back and it looked like it was going to sink!

Word Scrambles

Scramble	Clue	Numbered blanks
bimerst	(wood)	16, 27, 26, 36, 19
sirvonopsi	(supplies)	28, 14, 35, 29, 17
smocasp	(guide)	7, 18
spetmet	(storm)	2, 32, 1
urocusi	odd or unsual)	40, 6, 10, 20
fiedhsin	(done)	15, 4, 9
fosantifilc	(trials)	3, 8, 4, 22
gfedirenth	(scared)	34, 11, 33, 41, 5, 21, 25, 31
noweddr	(died in water)	23, 24, 30, 13, 12

What did they take on the ship?

1 Nephi 18:6

30 1   30 15 8 8   13 14 5   2 4 3 16

29 40 23   Y 7 20 25 33 12 6   27 11 24 2 4 21 28

17 41 18   8 8   27 9   3   36 40 8 32 23

22 35 31 36   20 19   *(This is what his elder brothers said about Nephi)*

BOOK OF MORMON ANIMALS

Can you put the animal names in the right places to make this puzzle work?

1 Nephi 18:25

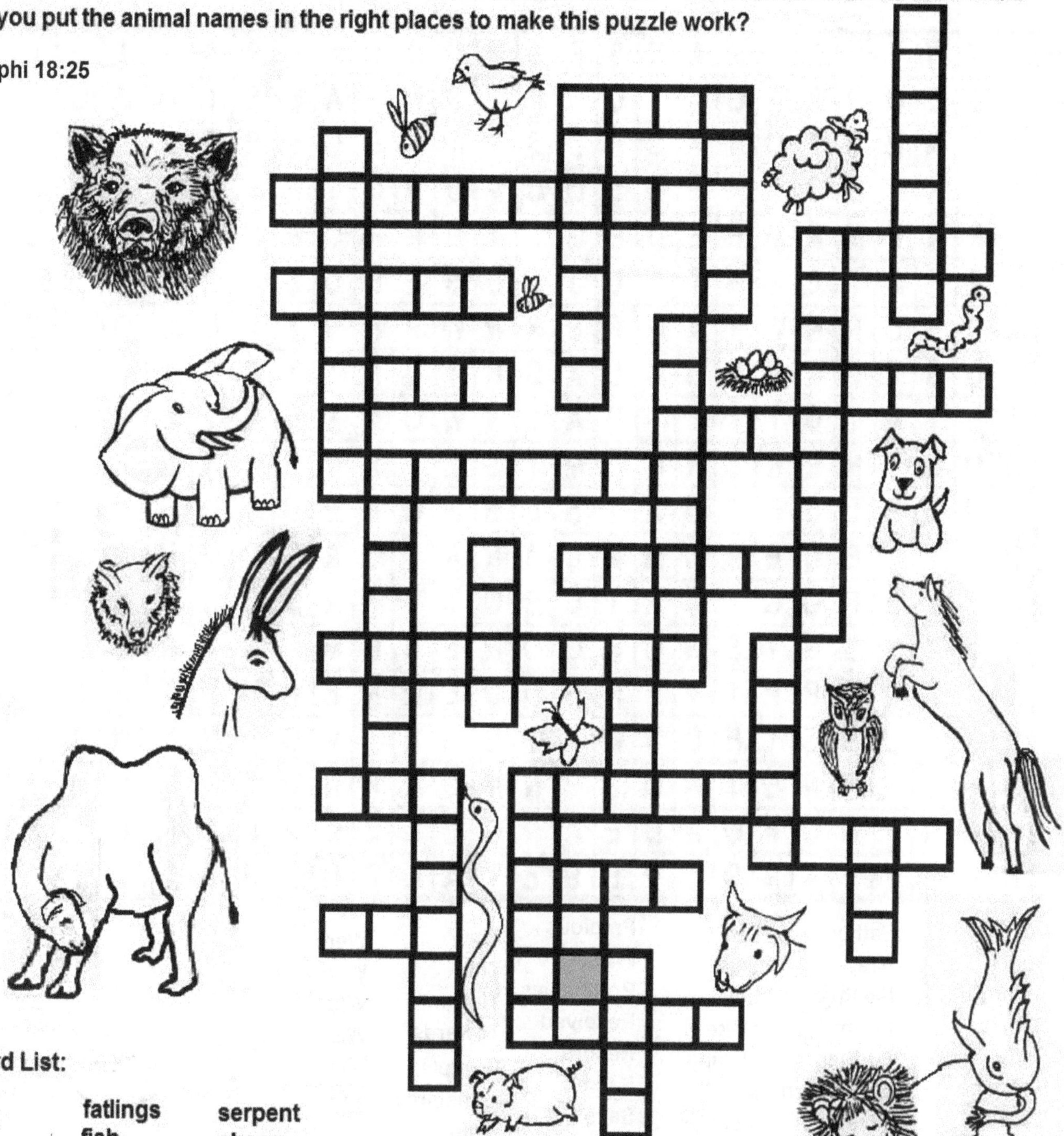

Word List:

asp
ass
bear
bittern
camel
cattle
cockatrice
cows
cumoms
curelom
dogs
elephant
fatlings
fish
goat
herds
honeybee
horses
lamb
leopards
lion
moth
owl
ox
serpent
sheep
swine
vultures
wildbeast
wolf
worm

Draw what you think cumoms and cureloms look like:

I Had Made These Plates...

I	H	W	T	H	T	T	R	A	N	S	P	I	R	E	D	K	A	E	P	S	N	I	A	L	P
G	U	E	H	P	S	N	O	I	T	C	U	R	T	S	N	I	A	E	S	I	W	O	U	L	D
E	N	A	E	C	P	O	A	F	S	H	D	S	M	I	T	E	C	E	R	O	F	E	B	C	D
N	D	K	Y	B	O	T	H	E	O	S	O	C	M	D	R	O	C	E	R	U	O	A	H	D	S
E	R	N	E	M	K	M	E	E	U	E	G	O	T	H	P	R	O	P	H	E	C	I	E	S	S
R	E	E	S	T	E	E	M	T	L	L	J	U	D	G	E	E	U	S	H	A	L	L	N	E	E
A	D	S	O	N	N	W	I	A	G	F	E	R	R	W	H	E	N	A	P	D	S	O	E	G	S
T	D	S	T	L	R	P	N	D	N	L	K	G	H	T	U	R	T	Y	R	O	I	J	R	A	S
I	L	I	A	I	D	T	I	L	I	D	A	E	N	W	O	N	K	E	E	T	E	E	G	D	O
O	O	O	T	H	E	R	S	R	K	E	M	Y	S	E	L	F	N	S	C	N	L	R	I	N	P
N	H	E	B	L	E	F	T	O	A	Y	S	E	S	W	W	A	E	U	I	U	P	U	V	O	C
D	E	V	I	E	C	E	R	W	M	R	C	A	N	A	Y	O	R	O	O	M	M	S	E	B	O
H	B	T	N	F	O	G	Y	C	A	I	C	B	O	T	V	T	R	M	U	N	A	A	S	F	U
A	U	X	I	S	R	Y	S	W	O	R	G	O	N	E	S	E	M	T	S	A	R	L	D	A	N
V	T	A	Q	M	P	P	I	V	E	N	H	D	D	E	E	R	E	W	H	U	T	E	R	T	S
E	X	C	U	S	E	T	H	D	N	W	A	Y	D	G	N	I	V	O	L	G	M	M	A	H	E
S	N	O	I	T	N	E	T	N	O	C	R	N	M	O	R	F	U	R	T	H	E	R	W	E	L
P	A	R	T	S	U	P	O	N	D	E	A	N	G	E	L	C	O	M	E	T	H	E	O	R	S
N	A	E	Y	E	A	R	S	T	V	L	S	E	T	A	L	P	H	E	R	E	A	F	T	E	R

Account
Angel
Before
Behold
Body
Bondage
Both
But
Children
Cometh
Commandment
Contentions
Counsels
Destructions
Done
Egypt
Err
Esteem
Excuse

Father
Feet
Flesh
From
Further
Generation
Gives
God
Gone
Have
Hereafter
Hundred
Iniquity
Instruction
Jerusalem
Judge
Kept
Known
Land

Left
Lord
Loving
Make
Making
Men
Mention
Ministry
Myself
Naught
New
Not
Old
Other
Our
Parts
Plain
Plates
Possess

Precious
Proceed
Prophecies
Received
Record
Sacred
Save
Say
Scourge
Shall
Six
Smite
Soul
Speak
Spoken

They
This
Time
Towards
Trample
Transpired
Truth
Unto
Upon
Very
Voices
Wars
Way
Weakness

Were
When
Who
Wise
World
Worth
Would
Write
Yea
Years

(extra letters go here)

The Crucifixion

Nephi quotes unknown prophets about the death of the Messiah

1 Nephi 19: 10-16

Zenock said he would be lifted up.

Neum said he would be crucified

Zenos tells of three days of darkness, thunderings, earthquakes and smoke

He would be buried in a sepulchre

I	E	L
Y		D
H	T	E

S	S	E
D		N
A	R	K

E	R	S
T		Q
R	A	U

C	S	D
O		E
U	R	G

P	I	S
S		E
E	D	D

R	R	E
E		B
M	E	M

Can you figure out these words from this page? They go in a circle and can go either way.

Answers:

Liken the Scriptures Unto Us

And he did surely show unto the prophets all things concerning them...they are written on the plates of brass

1 Nephi 19:21

Find words in criss-cross grids of five squares like this:

BRASS

S		B
	R	
A		S

The letters can be in any order.

Hint: Try picking a single letter and looking at the four letters that go with it and see if it makes a word. Many letters do!

Word List:

brass	Jacob	Moses	spake	truth
every	Judah	mouth	speak	weary
forth	lands	needs	swear	which
hosts	liken	sinew	teach	words
house	might	smite	those	would

These words can also be found in the puzzle:

hopes posse south
sneek saved spoof
other paper stash
stoke thank

S	W	F	D	R	S	U	B	O	T	U
T	P	R	H	V	T	R	R	A	D	B
O	S	O	E	T	A	H	S	W	J	L
L	S	E	E	Y	O	W	E	C	H	A
A	I	K	W	S	R	T	I	O	T	E
K	A	N	P	O	S	H	U	H	S	E
W	E	E	S	A	D	H	U	M	T	S
S	R	E	P	L	N	J	G	O	E	S
A	D	S	N	K	A	T	H	I	S	T

Peace Like A River

Nephi is sad, do you know why?

Can you find your way to the treasure through the waves of the sea?

O that thou hadst hearkened to my commandments - then had thy peace been as a river, thy righteousness as the waves of the sea. 1 Nephi 20: 19

the prophet isaiah

1 Nephi 21

God said to Isaiah:

"thou shouldst be my servant to raise up the tribes of Jacob and to restore ...Israel. I will also give thee for a light to the Gentiles..."

Can you fit all the four letter words into the puzzle?

Four-by-Four

ALSO	MADE
DAYS	NAME
DONE	ROCK
ENDS	SAID
EVEN	SAVE
EYES	SHOW
FEED	THAT
FLOW	THEE
FREE	THEM
FROM	THEY
GIVE	THIS
HAND	THOU
HATH	THUS
HAVE	TIME
HEAT	UNTO
HIGH	VAIN
HOLY	WAYS
LAST	WHOM
LEAD	WILL
LIKE	WITH
LIVE	WOMB
LORD	WORK

Nephi Quotes Isaiah

WORD LIST

Find all the words on the list on word chains snaking through the puzzle. Every letter will be used and some will be used more than once. One is marked for you as an example.

- Begotten
- Bind
- Bride
- Captive
- Desolate
- Destruction
- Eyes
- Fathers
- Forget
- Forth
- Heart
- Israel
- Lawful
- Mothers
- Narrow
- Nursing
- Prey
- Queens
- Waste

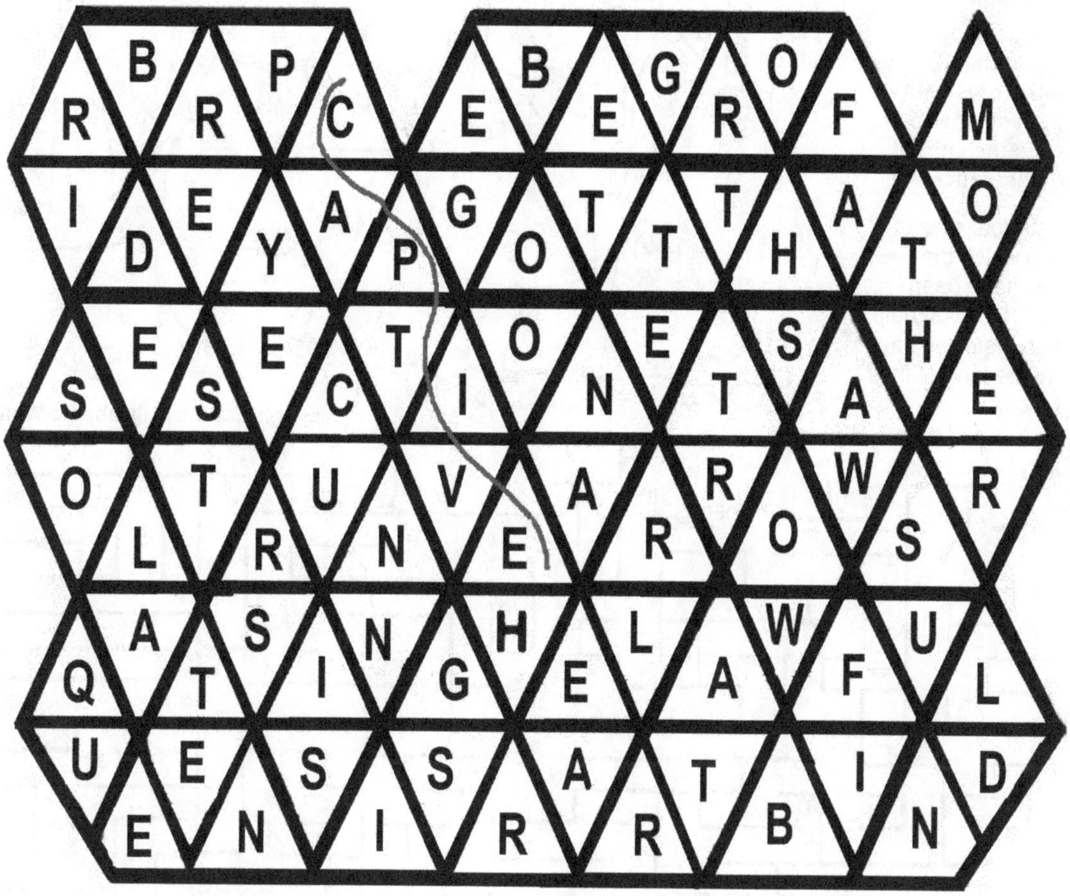

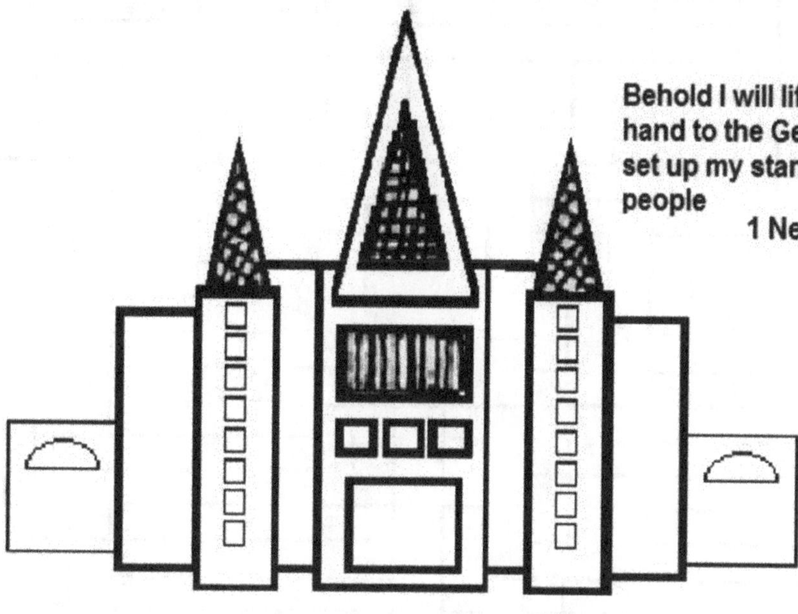

Behold I will lift up my hand to the Gentiles and set up my standard to my people

1 Nephi 21:22

Scattered Israel

1 Nephi 22:3

Nephi explains to his brothers that the people of Israel will be scattered among all the world. They were taken prisoner by conquerors as slaves, driven out of Israel.
But he reminds them that the Lord has promised that the scattered of Israel will be reclaimed a return to the land of their inheritance.

Below are four mazes of places to which the Israelites have been scattered. Can you help them find their way back home to the land of their inheritance?

In the Latter Days

WIL	ELO	A M
ARV	WOR	ROC
G T	HE	MON
US	L P	DO
EED	TO	K A

GOD ____ ________ ___ ___

__ __________ _____

_______ ____ **GENTILES**

Fill the blanks with the word sections in the squares above to see what it says.

1 Nephi 22: 51

1 Nephi 22:25

FUTURE DAYS

R	E	W	H	A	T	S	O	E	V	E	R	M	O	D	G	N	I	K	N	O	W
E	E	X	S	S	D	H	P	H	A	F	T	D	E	D	N	U	O	F	N	O	C
S	R	W	E	R	S	E	R	T	R	F	O	L	D	N	E	R	D	L	I	H	C
T	A	A	O	C	Q	A	O	E	M	I	T	U	S	E	V	L	A	C	N	N	R
A	L	W	O	P	U	R	P	R	B	N	G	W	R	P	Y	D	O	F	F	E	E
B	C	M	W	G	A	T	H	E	R	E	T	H	I	H	F	E	E	D	L	D	F
L	E	L	H	N	R	S	E	B	E	S	O	H	T	I	A	S	S	F	P	R	F
I	D	H	O	A	T	U	T	M	T	H	U	S	G	E	S	T	O	O	V	A	U
S	W	I	C	K	E	D	L	U	H	D	E	E	N	I	O	R	P	E	E	H	S
H	Z	N	F	I	R	E	O	N	R	U	P	O	N	W	F	U	L	N	E	S	S
E	E	I	N	A	S	M	O	K	E	E	O	I	D	R	L	C	S	C	U	T	P
D	P	Q	M	O	C	W	S	E	N	R	A	E	F	A	T	T	B	N	S	S	E
L	M	U	U	E	K	E	E	R	A	G	V	S	R	T	R	I	E	U	E	I	R
R	A	I	S	A	V	E	D	P	D	R	N	A	B	H	E	O	L	S	N	S	I
O	N	T	T	A	K	O	E	N	E	E	T	Y	U	S	M	N	O	T	E	H	S
W	N	Y	P	A	O	E	O	S	V	O	S	H	I	E	B	M	N	E	M	D	H
I	E	O	P	L	I	K	E	E	I	W	P	O	L	L	L	S	G	N	I	H	T
L	R	S	B	I	S	R	A	E	L	A	A	L	T	F	E	N	G	I	E	R	A
L	A	E	R	A	P	E	R	P	Y	S	R	Y	E	L	B	B	U	T	S	I	H

"and He numbereth His sheep,and they know Him; and there shall be one fold and one Shepherd;and he shall feed His sheep, and in Him they shall find pasture."

When you have found all the words, the remaining letters will say:

WORD LIST:

Belong
Blood
Brethren
Built
Calves
Children
Come
Confoundec
Cut
Declare
Destruction
Devil
Dust
Earth
Enemies
Established
Even
Execute
Eyes
Face
Fear
Feed
Fight
Fine
Fire
Flesh
Fold
For
Four
Fulness
Gain
Gathereth
Harden
Hath
Hearts
His
Holy
Iniquity
Israel
Kingdom
Know
Like
Loosed
Lord
Low
Lusts

Manner
Moses
Must
Need
Nephi
Numbereth
Off
Pass
Pasture
People
Perish
Popular
Power
Prepared
Preserved
Prophet
Quake
Quarters
Raise
Reign
Righteousness
Saith
Saved
Say
Seek
Sheep Sin
Smoke
Spake
Stubble
Suffer
Things
Those
Thus
Time
Tremble
Upon
Vapor
Way
Whatsoever
Who
Wicked
Will
Words
Wrath
Zion

Jerusalem is Destroyed!

"...had we remained in Jerusalem, we should also have been destroyed."

2 Nephi 1:5

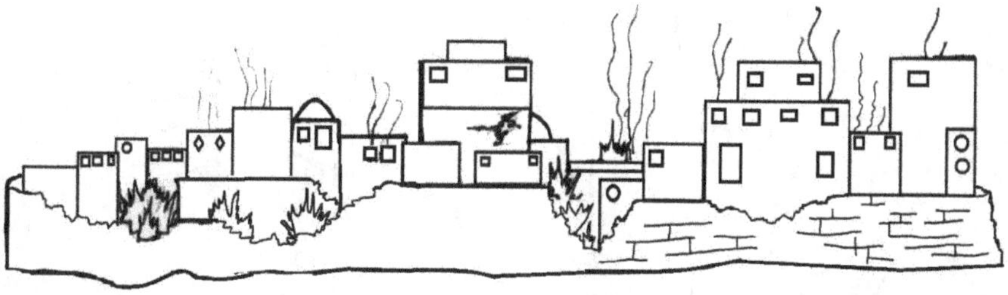

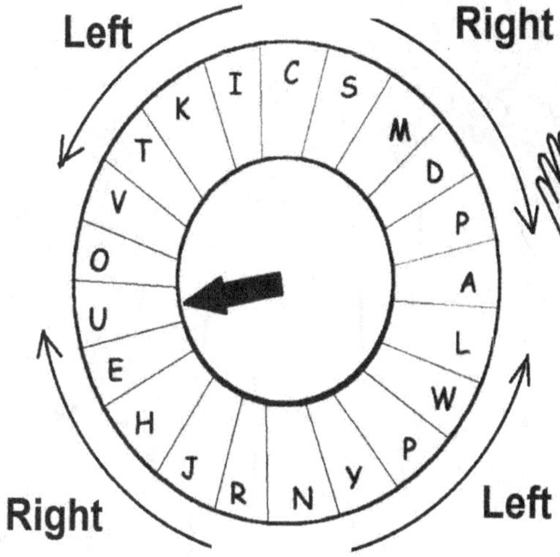

DIRECTIONS: Start at the arrow point.
Go Left or Right as many spaces as directed.
(Left is counter-clockwise and right is clockwise.)
Write down that letter and go on to the next one,
as if you were doing a combination lock.
If you do this correctly you will see the message
that Lehi gave to his sons!

R5 | L7 L8 L9 L3 | R8 L8 L0 L4 | L5

L9 R3 R2 L2 L4 L6 | L11 R11 | L3 R6 R7 R1 L8

R7 | L1 L9 R6 L9 | L10 L5 L8 L8

L6 R2 L3 R4 R7 R4 R1 R8 R9 | L3 R2

R2 R11 R8 L4 L7 R5 L7 R5 R10

Lehi Counsels His Children

HIDDEN PICTURES - Can you find:
duck, fish, mouse, turtle, seahorse, rabbit, 2 sheep, 2 birds, 3 snakes, tooth axe, broom, bell, knife, fork, spoon, horn, jingle bell, cowry shell, sailboat, 2 keys

2 Nephi 1:7

Lehi tells his children that this land is consecrated to those he brings to dwell in it, and if they will serve him and keep his commandments they will be blessed, and prospered and it will be a land of liberty to them, but if they do not, they will eventually be swept off.

Shake Off Those Chains!

2 Nephi 1:23

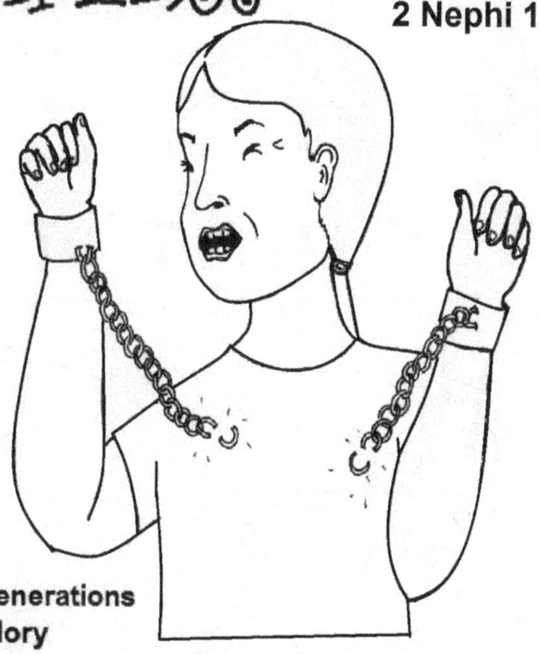

Lehi was dying and he pleaded with his rebellious sons to choose righteousness and not to be hateful to their brother Nephi.....

WORDCHAINS

Find all the words below in the wordchains. Letters can touch at the top or bottom or either side, but not diagonally, and they will twist all around. One has been done for you as an example.

Anxiety
Arise
Armor
Arms
Been
But

Captivity
Chains
Choice
Cold
Cursing
Cut

Days
Desire
Destroyed
Devil
Down
Dust

Encircled
Famine
Favored
Feared
Forever
Fulness

Generations
Glory
Grave
Hands
Hunger
Lord

Incur
Instrument
Jerusalem
Judgment

Limbs
Lived
Love
Might
Mind
Needs
Obscurity
Off Out
Parent Path
Promise
Redeemed
Righteousness
Silent
Sons
Sore
Sorrow
Soul
Sword
Things
Views
Ways
Wilderness
Words
Wrath
Ye

```
    F R O W D           N E S S G
   F O R Y E N I   I H U S O I C E N
 C U S O V E D M A S R O C H M N G E R
 H T G L I B U T F A M E I A O U Y A A
 V A R E A D C R E R I T N I R H S W T
 E P W N Y J O L D I G H C N P D R I I
 G A H T S U D I E S E R U S I F O L O
 N N D S T U G M E N J S R A L U L D N
 I S A R M O R B M T B O U L E L O E S
   R U C I R C L E C S O N E N N V R
   F E N A D E S D U T Y S M T E E N
     A X I E R T R R I V I E W S S
     R E E T O W O Y S G N I H T Y
       D O Y V S I E D E N T V I
         W N A F N S U M P T I
              S O R T R C A
                  E V E
```

ANGRY BROTHERS

2 Nephi 1:26

Laman and Lemuel accuse Nephi of seeking for power and...

Follow the paths to put the letters in the right order

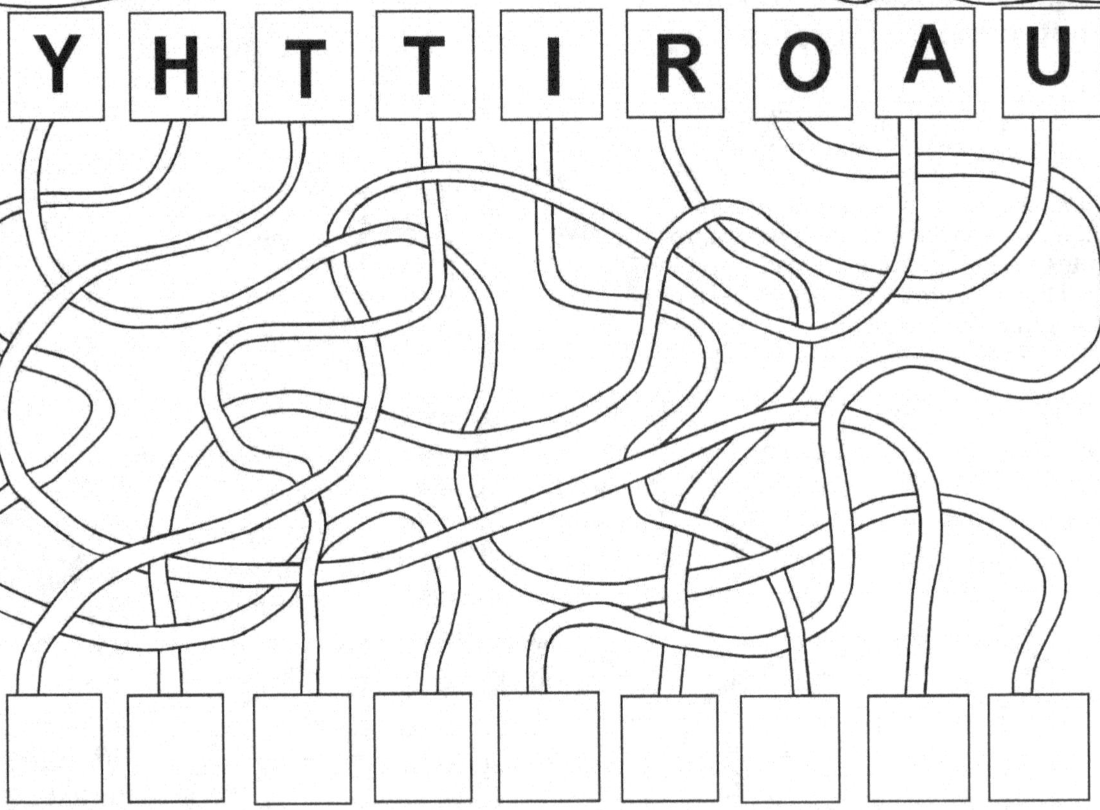

Lehi told them that he did not seek it, but that God had chosen him because of his faith and obedience.

Can you draw what they did next? (the usual)

The Light of Christ

2 Nephi 2:5

(Tip the paper at an angle and the word on the candle will be read easily)

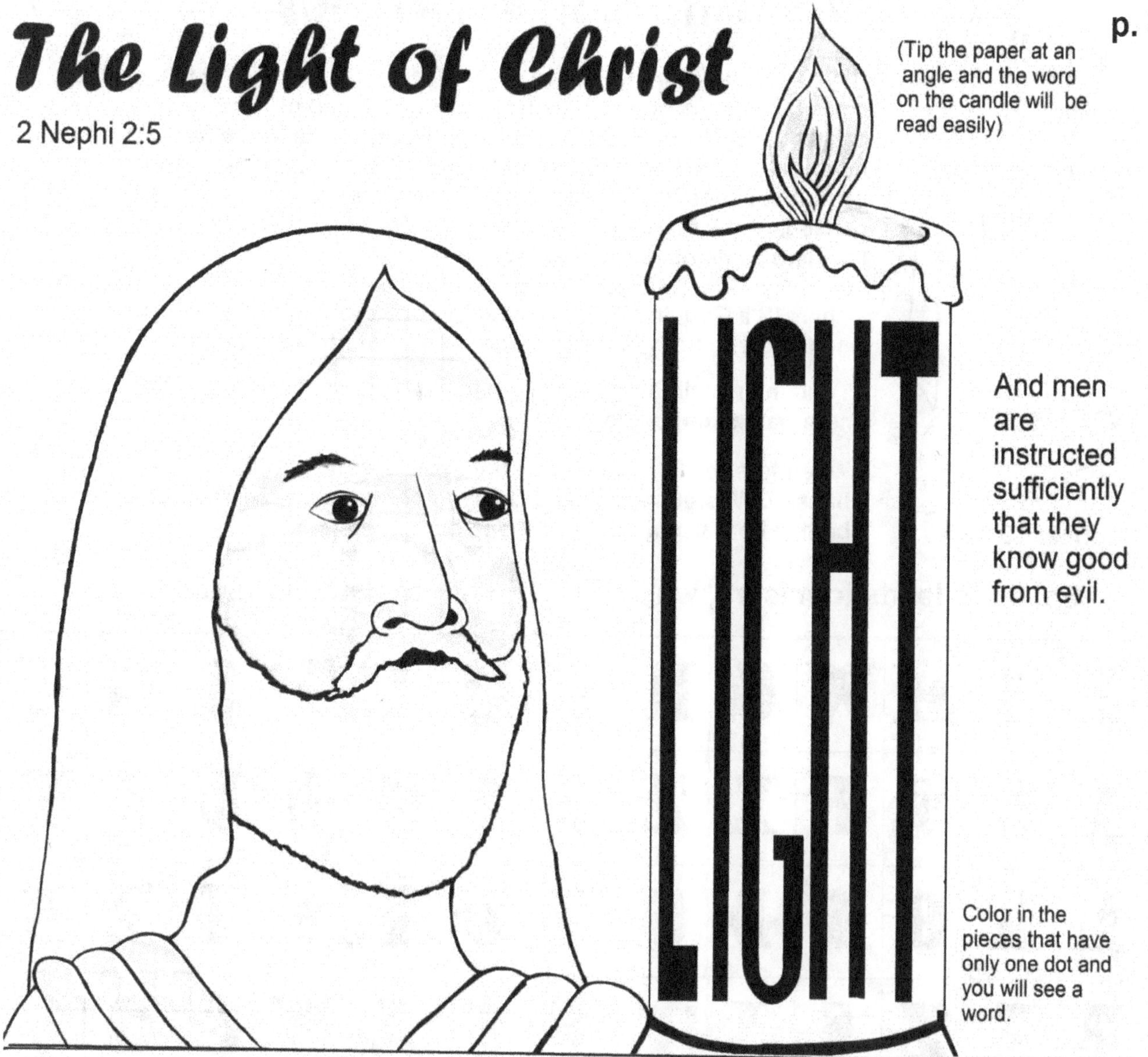

And men are instructed sufficiently that they know good from evil.

Color in the pieces that have only one dot and you will see a word.

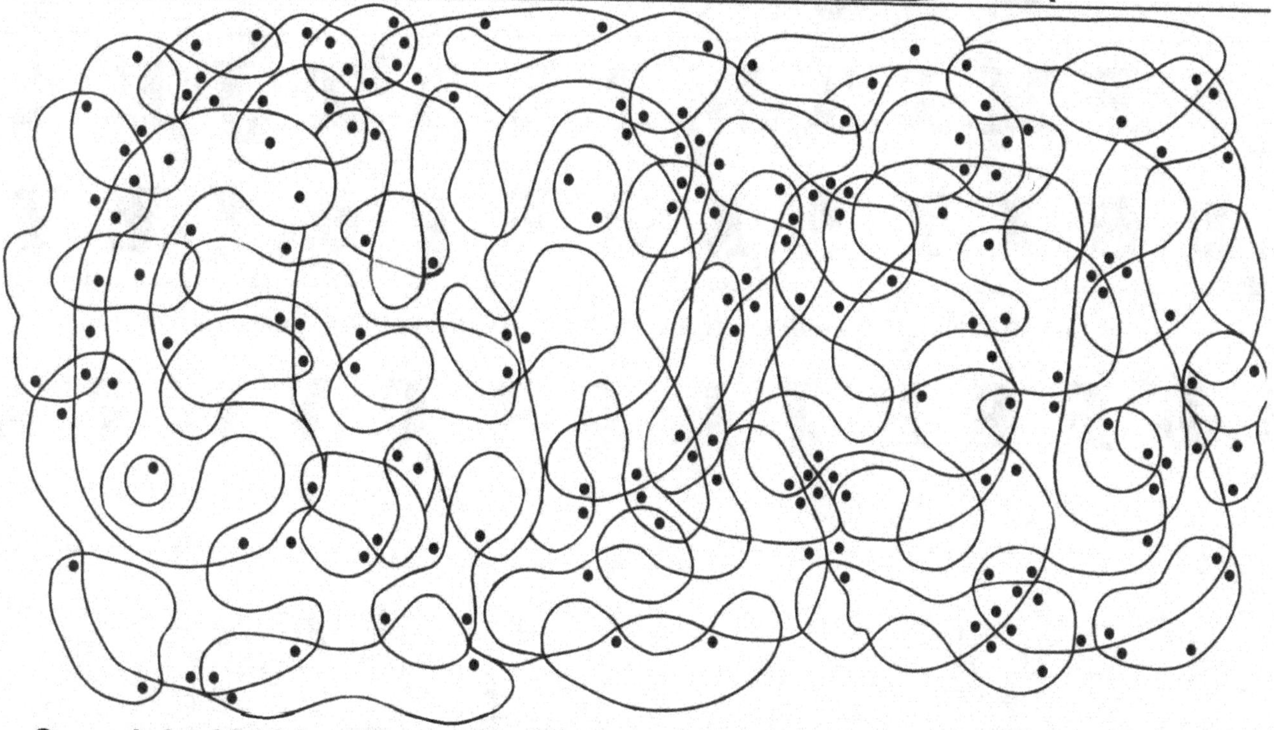

Opposition In All Things

2 Nephi 2: 13-16

"If ye shall say there is no law, ye shall also say there is no sin. If ye shall say there is no sin, ye shall also say there is no righteousness. And if there be no righteousness there be no happiness. And if there be no righteousness nor happiness, there be no punishment nor misery. And if these things are not, there is no God. And if there is no God, then we are not, neither the earth; for there could have been no creation...

...there IS a God and he hath created all things, both the heavens and the earth..both things to act and things to be acted upon...

... and in fine, all things which are created, it must needs be that there was an opposition...

Wherefore the Lord God gave unto man that he should act for himself. Wherefore man could not act for himself save it should be that he was enticed by the one or the other.....

So, if sin leads to misery, why would Satan be enticing us all to sin?

F	J	M	W	G	K	F	H	I	T	S	H	U
T	U	V	E	X	Z	R	Q	W	D	U	B	Y
L	K	G	T	D	O	K	U	F	V	T	Z	X
B	E	Z	S	J	T	F	C	Z	W	G	O	V
V	B	M	D	T	W	P	U	X	T	J	K	A
D	G	X	T	Q	N	G	F	D	G	Y	Z	F

Cross out all the letters below in the boxes above and you will see a message:

B D F G H J K Q T U V W Y Z

__________ _________ _____________

Color me!

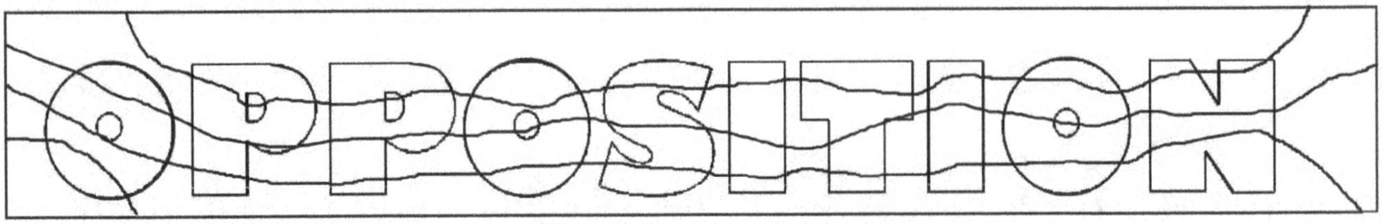

The Purpose of Life

Can you find the missing pieces?

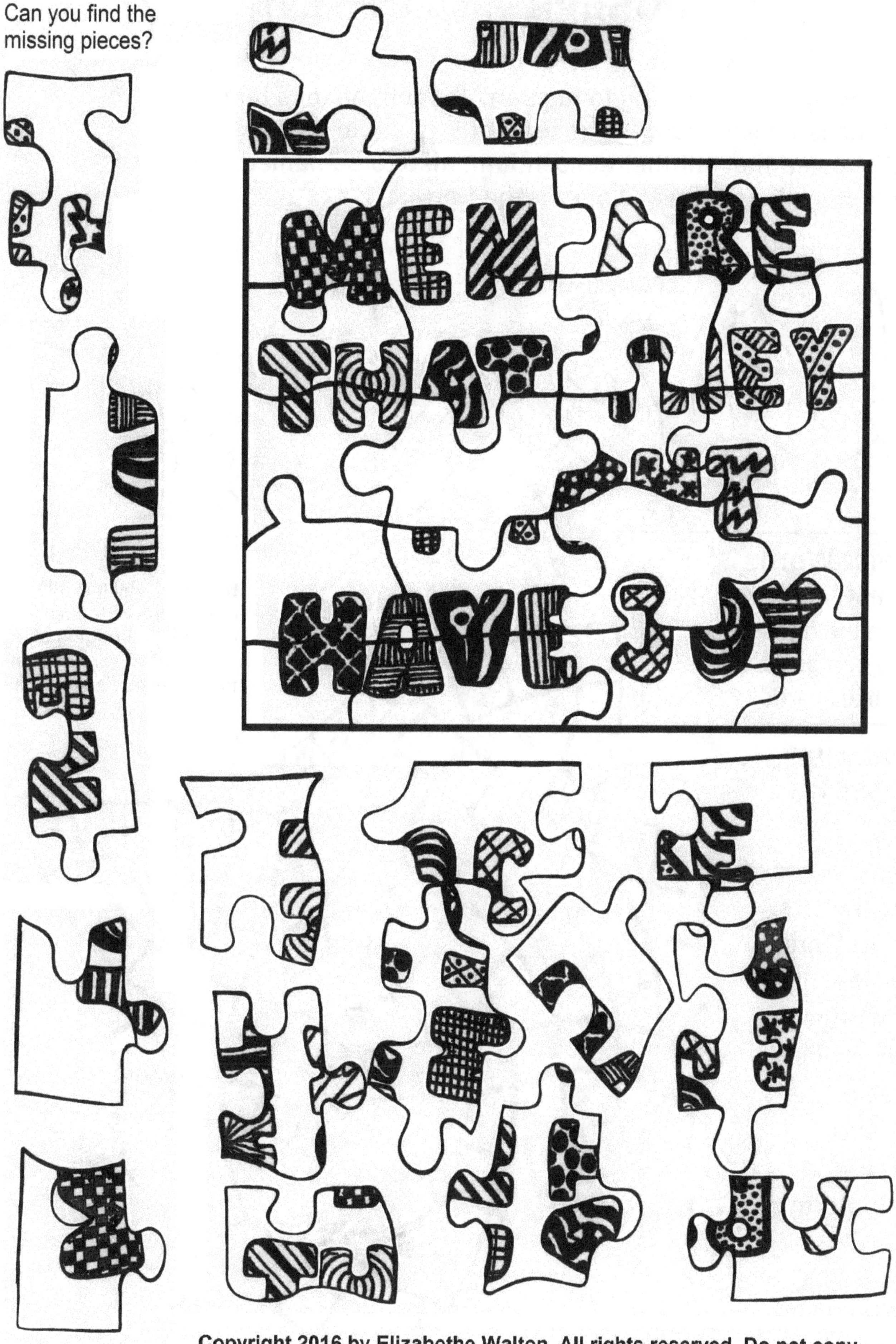

Joseph and Joseph

As Lehi gives a blessing to his son, Joseph, he tells him that he is a descendant of Joseph of Egypt and that he prophesied that another descendant, also to be named Joseph, will do a great work for the Lord.

Twist-Words

Put the words from the list in the right slots. They can go forwards or backwards.

2 N

He shall do a work for the fruit of thy loins, his brethren, which shall be of great worth unto them, even to the bringing of them to the knowledge of the covenants which I have made with thy fathers.

WORD LIST:
be brethren
bringing
covenants do
even fathers.
for fruit great
have he his
knowledge
loins made
of shall the
thy unto
which with
work worth

2 Nephi 3:12

Two Sticks

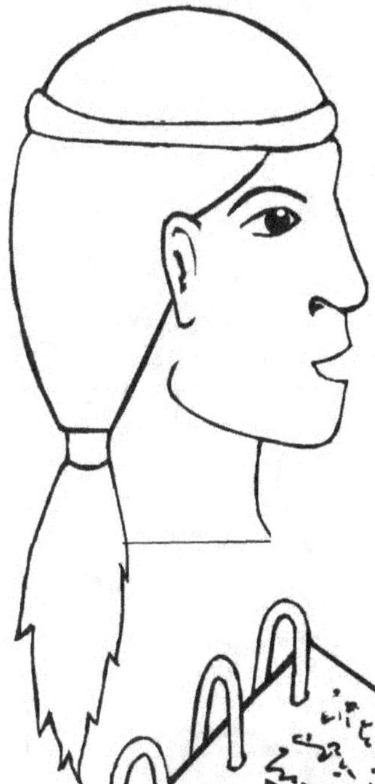

Can you fill in the missing vowels to see what this says?

Wh__r__f__r__ th__
fr__ __t __f th__ l__ __ns
sh__ll wr__t__; __nd
th__ fr__ __t __f th__
l__ __ns __f J__d__h
sh__ll wr__t__; __ nd
th__t wh__ch sh__ll b__
wr__tt__n sh__ll gr__w
t__g__th__r __nt__ th__
c__nf__ __nd__ng __f
f__ls__ d__ctr__n__s
__nd l__y__ng d__wn
__f c__nt__nt__ __ns.

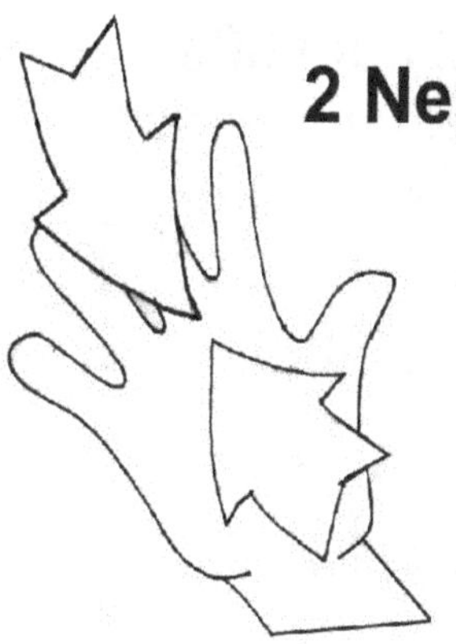

2 Nephi 3:12

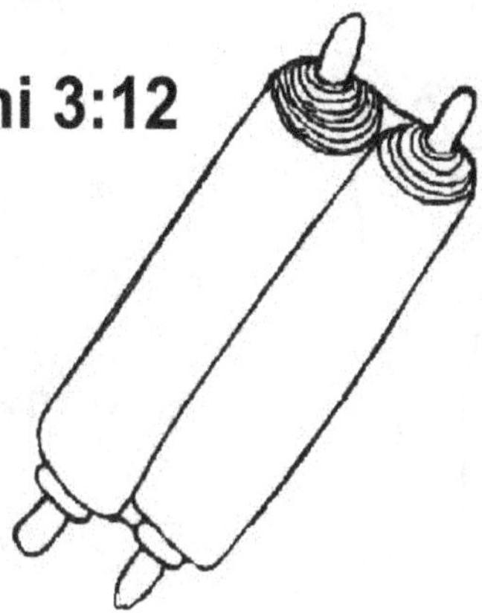

Remember that E is the most common vowel in the English language, so try that one first. Then you may see a word forming that will clue you in to what the others are.

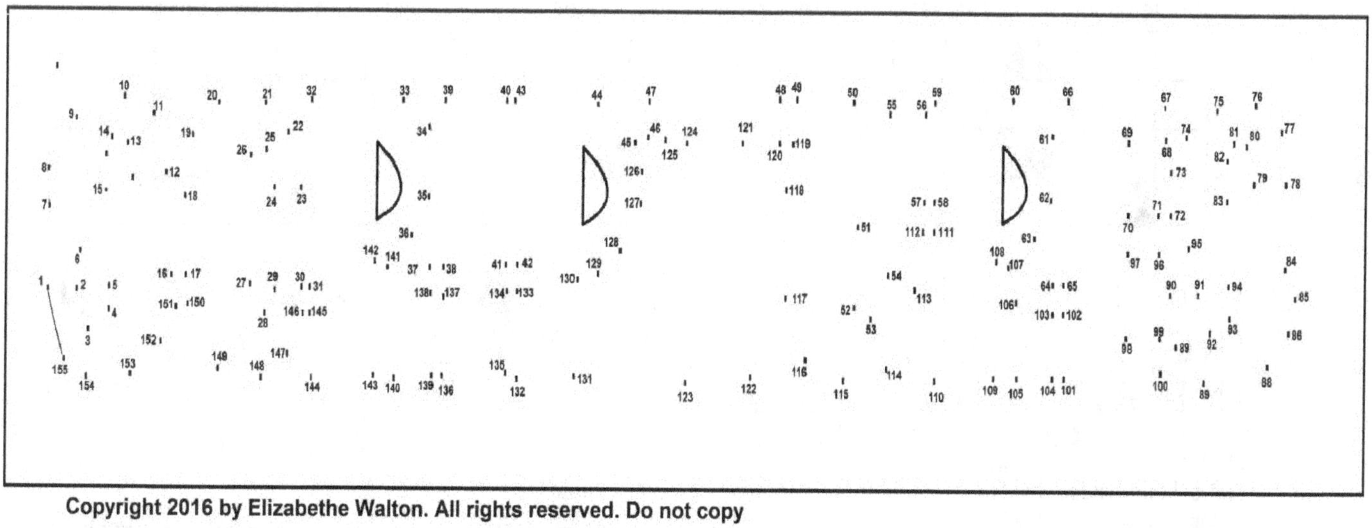

A PROMISE TO THE LAMANITES

2 Nephi 3:24

Wherefore, if ye are cursed, behold, I leave my blessing upon you, that the cursing may be taken from you and be answered upon the heads of your parents. Wherefore because of my blessing, the Lord God will not suffer that ye shall perish: Wherefore he will be merciful unto you and your seed forever.

2 Nephi 4:6-7

Wordfall Puzzle - In each column place the letters in the correct places to make a saying from the scriptures

					■						■					■			■				■
M						■						■					■				■	■	■
S					■			■					■	G				...	U				■
			■					■		F	■				■								N

Letters

M	H	A	H	L	Y	S	H	A	L	F	C	T	I	G	O	B	R	P	H	H	T	E	N
S	H	G	L	E	E	E	O	M	O	L	G	H	T	Y	E	O	U	E	U	O	R	E	
T	H	E	R	T		D	D		O	U		R	H	S	E	M	D	W	T	O	N	O	
T	I	E		S			A		M	N				H						N			

In the last column, There Is only 1 letter, so that one is obvious, and a couple more have been done for you.

Nephi Loves...

2 Nephi 4: 15

...for my soul delighteth in the scriptures, and my heart pondereth them and writeth them for the learning and profit of my children.

There are two messages in the text below. For the first, start with the second letter and choose every other letter.

For the other message, start with the first letter and choose every other letter and then add the words " the wilderness" at the end.

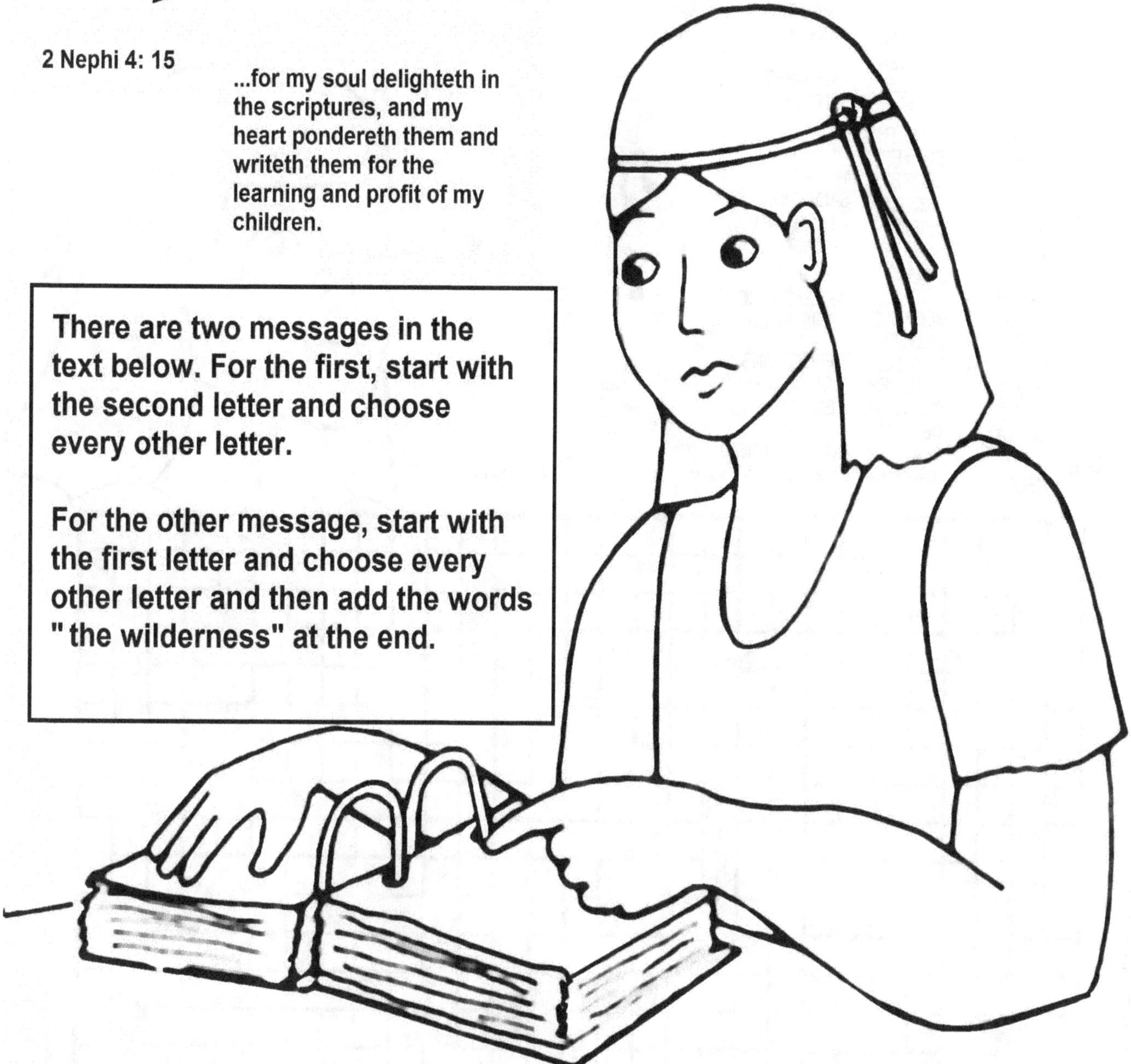

M A Y N G D O U D P H O A N T T H H B E E S E E
N I M W Y R S I U T P E P T O H R E T T H H E I
H N A G T S H O L F E M D Y M S E O T U H L R A
O N U D G M H A M N I Y N O E F A T F H F E L S
I C C R T I I P O T N U S R I E N S - the wilderness

The Psalm of Nephi

3
ARE
ARM
ASK
HIS
NOT
SIN
THE
YEA

4
BODY
EVEN
EYES
HATH
HIGH
KNOW
MAKE
MINE
PATH
ROAD
ROBE
SHUT
SOUL
THEE
THEN
THIS
UPON
WEEP

5
CLEAR
DROOP
GATES
GREAT
HANDS
HEART
HEDGE
MERCY
PLACE
PLAIN
SHAKE
WASTE
YIELD

6
ASKETH
BIDDEN
BROKEN
CURSED
LINGER
MAKETH
PRAYER
SECRET
SHOULD
SPIRIT
STRICT
VALLEY

7
BECAUSE
DELIVER
ENEMIES
FOREVER
PUTTETH
REJOICE
SLACKEN
TRUSTED

8
CHILDREN
CONTRITE
ENCIRCLE
STRAIGHT
STRENGTH

9
LIBERALLY
MOUNTAINS
SALVATION
STUMBLING
THEREFORE

10
APPEARANCE
MINISTERED

11
AFFLICTIONS
CONTINUALLY
TEMPTATIONS

13
CONDESCENSION
RIGHTEOUSNESS

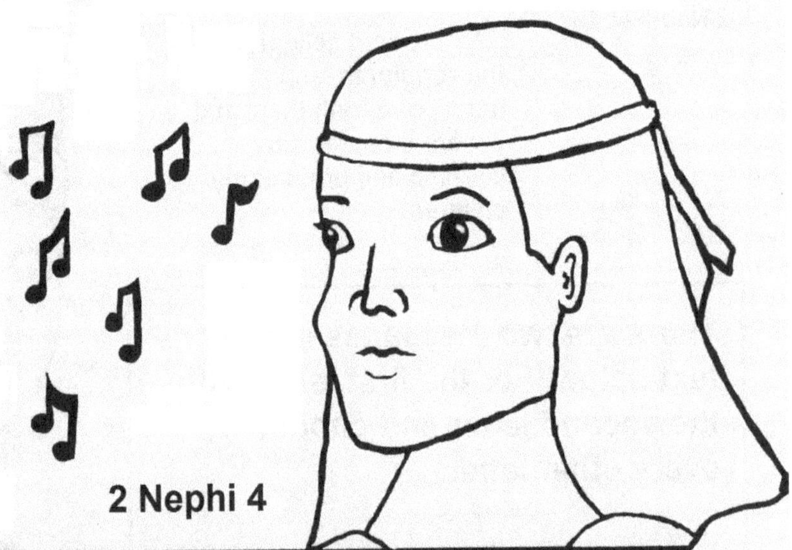

2 Nephi 4

LAMANITES AND NEPHITES

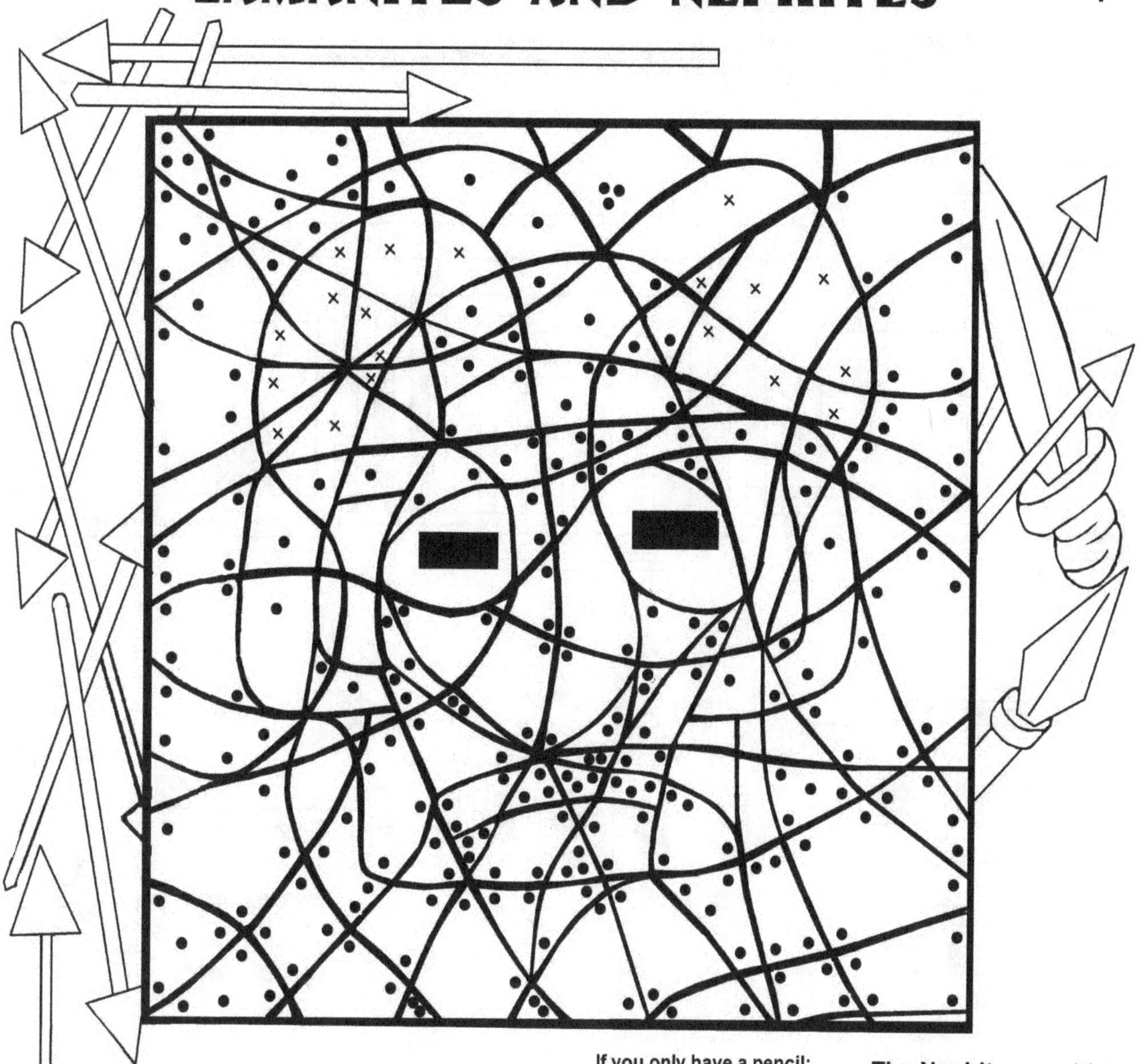

The Lamanites became wicked and persecuted the Nephites

Jacob 7:26

	If you only have a pencil:
● color yellow or orange	light gray
●● color gray or brown	medium gray
●●● color red	dark gray
x color blue	black

If you color the picture correctly you will see something!

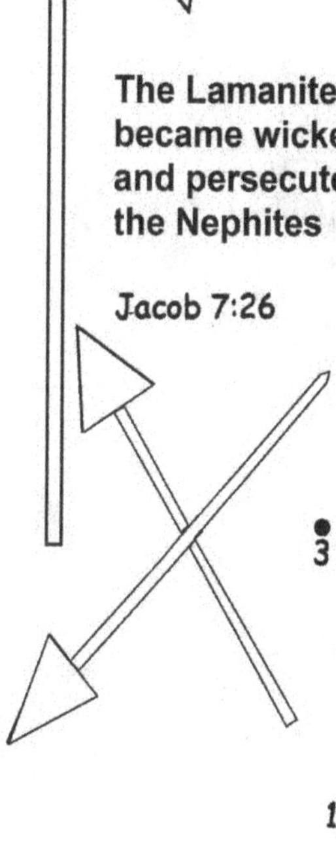

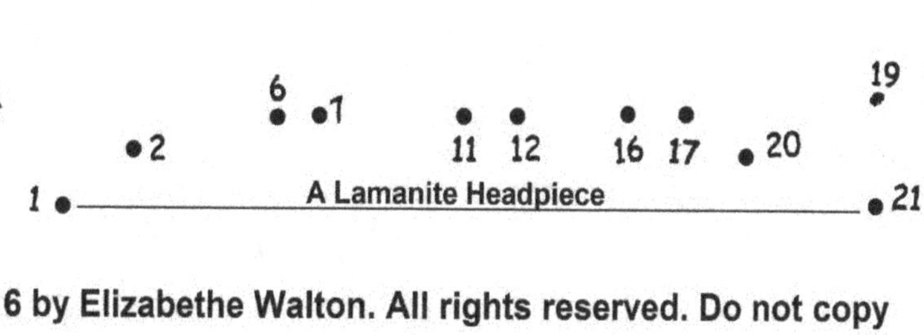

The Nephites went to Zarahemla and joined the Mulekites who came from Jerusalem after it was destroyed.

The Nephites and the Mulekites joined to one nation under King Mosiah.

But they had no brass plates and had forgotten how to read and write and keep the laws of God.

The Nephites Prosper

And I did teach my people to build buildings and to work in all manner of wood and of iron and of copper and of brass and of steel and of gold and of silver and of precious ores.

And I Nephi, did build a temple...

Draw your own house here:

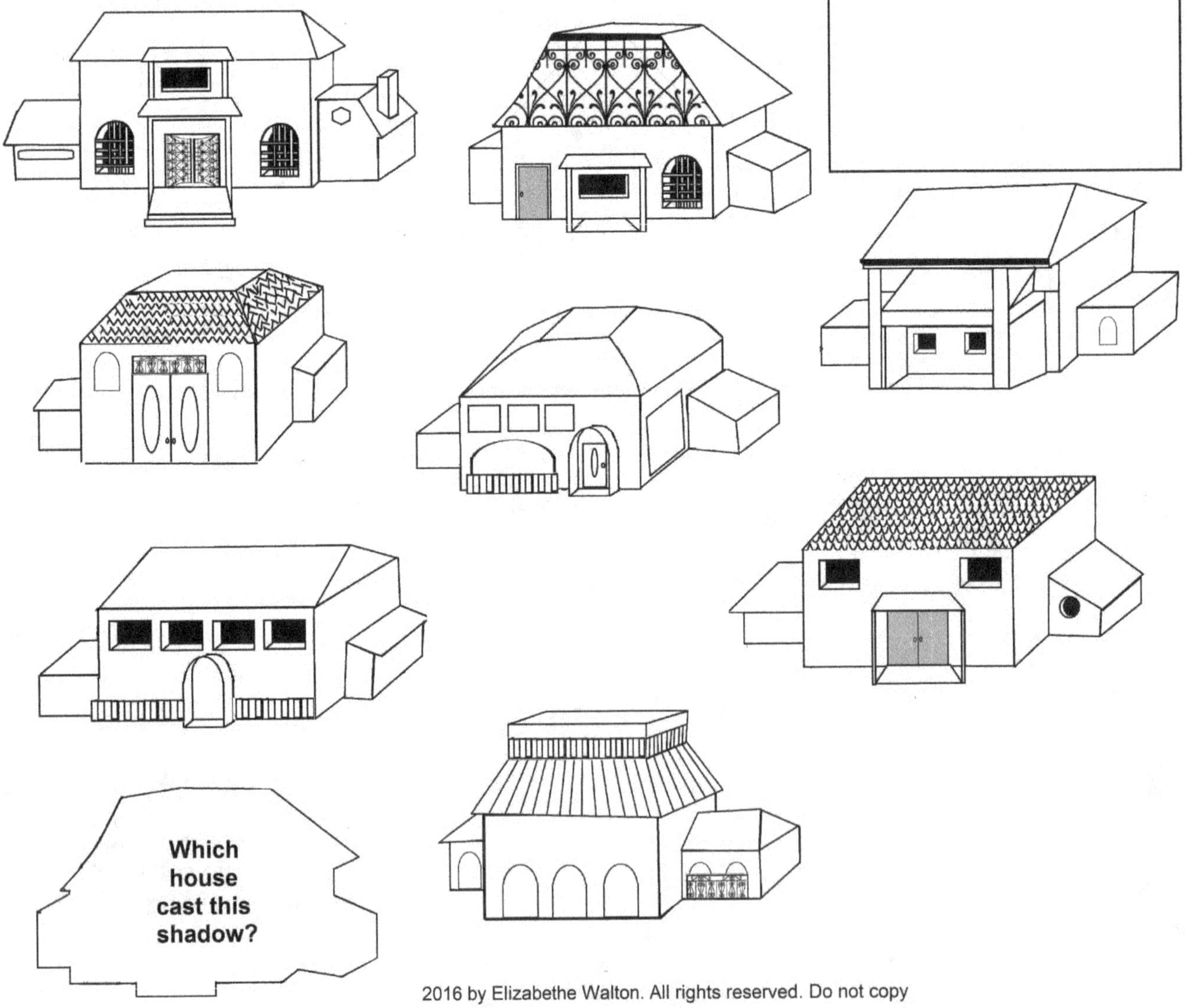

Consecrated Brothers

...having been consecrated by my brother Nephi.....

2 Nephi 6:2

Fit the words from the word list below into the puzzle

WORD LIST

3
God

4
Holy
Many
Name
Read
Sins

5
Learn
Souls

6
Behold
Called
Depend
Isaiah
Safety
Spoken
Taught

7
Brother
Desired
Glorify
Welfare
Written

8
Brethren
Exhorted
Diligence
Ministry
Obedient
Ordained

9
Concerned

11
Consecrated
Exceedingly

13
Commandments

Kings Shall Be Thy Nursing Fathers

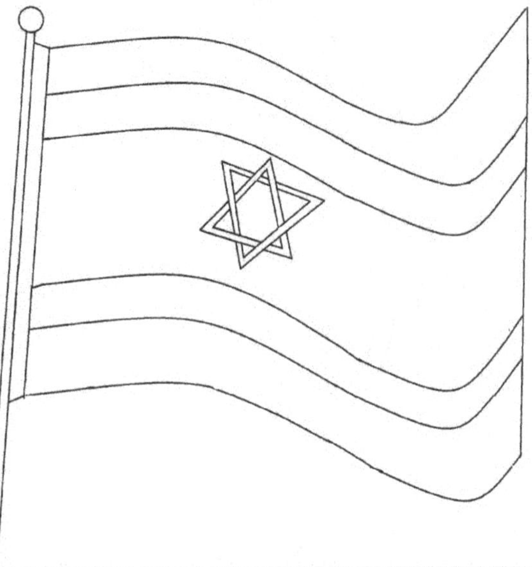

The flag of Israel is white with two blue stripes and a blue Star of David in the middle.

In 1948 King George the VI of Britain, with the support of many world leaders returned the land of Israel to the Jews, thus fulfilling this prophecy.

2 Nephi 6:6-7

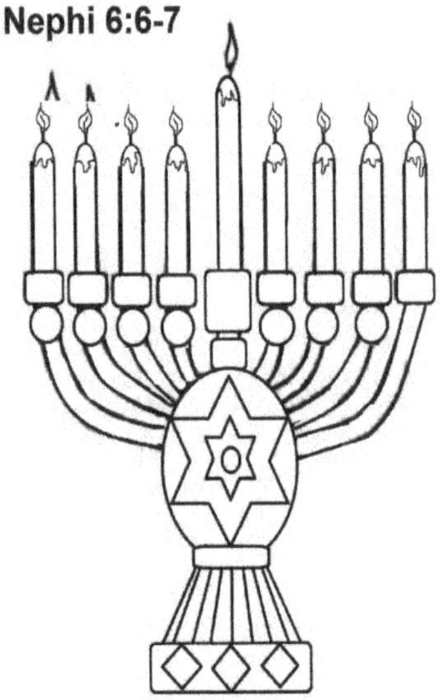

Cross out all the following to see a message:
A and I in EVEN numbered COLUMNS
P except on the 2nd ROW
S except on the last ROW
R on all EVEN numbered ROWS
W on all the ODD numbered ROWS
S in COLUMN 5
R in COLUMN 13 and 17
N in column 4
and all these: J K Q U V X Y Z

F	V	O	Z	J	W	R	P	U	I	K	Y	T	Z	U	Q	H	J	Q	A	P	E	V	X
Y	P	R	E	X	A	S	K	O	R	P	A	L	S	E	Q	X	O	K	Z	F	R	Q	T
Z	U	H	I	W	E	V	J	Q	X	Y	L	W	O	V	A	W	R	J	S	Z	D	K	A
W	S	X	Y	A	K	R	S	I	V	Q	U	S	J	S	I	P	T	U	R	F	S	J	O
R	V	T	A	P	W	U	H	K	A	W	E	R	C	W	Q	R	A	S	O	Y	M	P	V
I	Q	J	N	Q	X	P	G	Z	R	J	O	P	Z	F	R	Y	T	Z	Q	X	P	H	J
Z	E	P	Y	S	I	M	U	Y	E	J	I	X	S	S	X	P	V	I	K	A	I	W	H

Messiah Will Come

A: 2B, 5J, 6D, 7H, 8B, 10C
E: 1B, 2F, 3E, 4H, 5G, 6C, 7C, 8H, 9C, 9H, 10H, 10K, 10M,
I: 1E, 2D, 3B, 5A, 10J, 11A, 11E
0: 4D, 5E, 6I, 8F
U: 4A
B: 10G
C: 8E
D: 5L, 8A
F: 2E, 3G
G: 6A, 6G
H: 1A, 3A, 4G, 7B, 7G, 8J, 9B, 9G, 10B, 11D
L:1F, 1G, 3F, 6H, 10D, 10E, 10I
M: 2A, 3C, 4I, 8G, 11F,
N: 2C, 4B, 5B, 5K, 7D, 9D, 11B
P: 5D
R: 5H, 6B, 6J
S; 2G, 3D, 10A
T: 2H, 4C, 4F, 6E, 7F, 7I, 8I, 9F
V: 10L
W: 1D, 5F, 7A, 9A
Y: 6K, 8C, 9I

Using the grid coordinates, plot each letter into the correct place and you will see a message.

	A	B	C	D	E	F	G	H	I	J	K	L	M
1													
2													
3													
4													
5													
6													
7													
8													
9													
10													
11													

I WILL COMFORT HER WASTE PLACES

2 Nephi 8:3

HIDDEN PICTURES
Can you find a button, candle, deer, fork, bacon and eggs, spoon brush, knife, key , fish

They Shall Come to Zion

2 Nephi 8:11

Therefore, the redeemed of the Lord shall return, and come singing unto Zion; and everlasting joy and holiness shall be upon their heads; and they shall obtain gladness and joy; sorrow and mourning shall flee away.

Christ:

Pleadeth the _ _ _ ◯ _ of his people

Laid the _ _ _ _ _ ◯ _ _ _ _ of the earth

Brings everlasting joy and _ _ ◯ _ _ _ _ _ _

Righteousness shall be _ _ _ _ _ ◯ _ _

The Lord thy _ ◯ _ _ _

Made the _ _ _ ◯ _ _ of the sea a way for the ransomed to pass over

They shall _ _ _ _ _ ◯ _ gladness

Have covered thee with the _ _ _ _ _ ◯ _ of mine hand

Sorrow and _ _ _ _ _ ◯ _ _ _ shall flee away

The word is Christ's great gift to us:

_ _ _ _ _ _ _ _ _ _

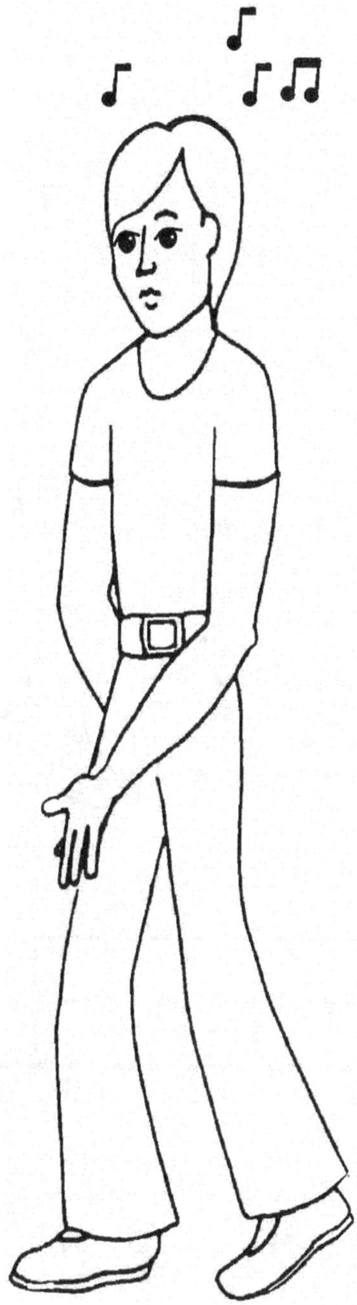

Find the missing words by reading

2 Nephi 8:-22

and fill them in.

Then the circled letters will make a word that is very important for us.

HE WILL COME IN THE BODY

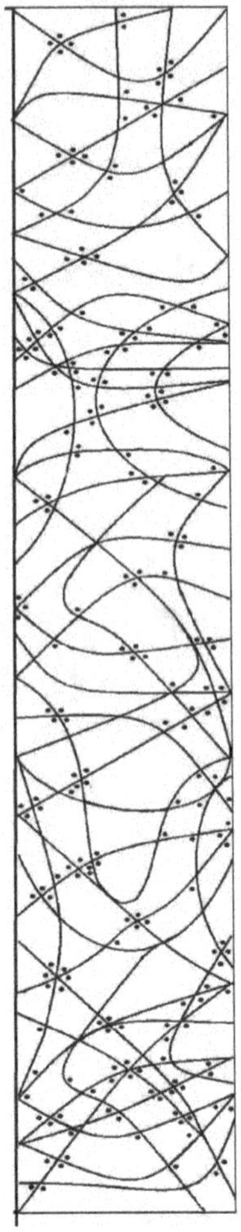

...he shall show himself unto those at Jerusalem, from whence we came, for...he suffereth himself to become subject unto man in the flesh, and die for all men, that all men might become subject unto him.

2 Nephi 9:5

Color in those segments that have two dots to see something.

The letters which belong to each column are below that column, but jumbled. You will need to figure out which letters go where to figure out what the puzzle says.

WORDFALL

W	H	F	R	S	I	B	E	E	A	T	T	N	M	U	S	T	T
I	E	E	I	E	F	O	R		A	I	O		E	M	E	N	
N	N	E	D	N		T	E			N							

The Spirit and the Body

Jacob teaches about death and resurrection and that we will all be redeeemed from death because of Christ's atonement, and then we will face the judgment of God.

2 Nephi 9:4

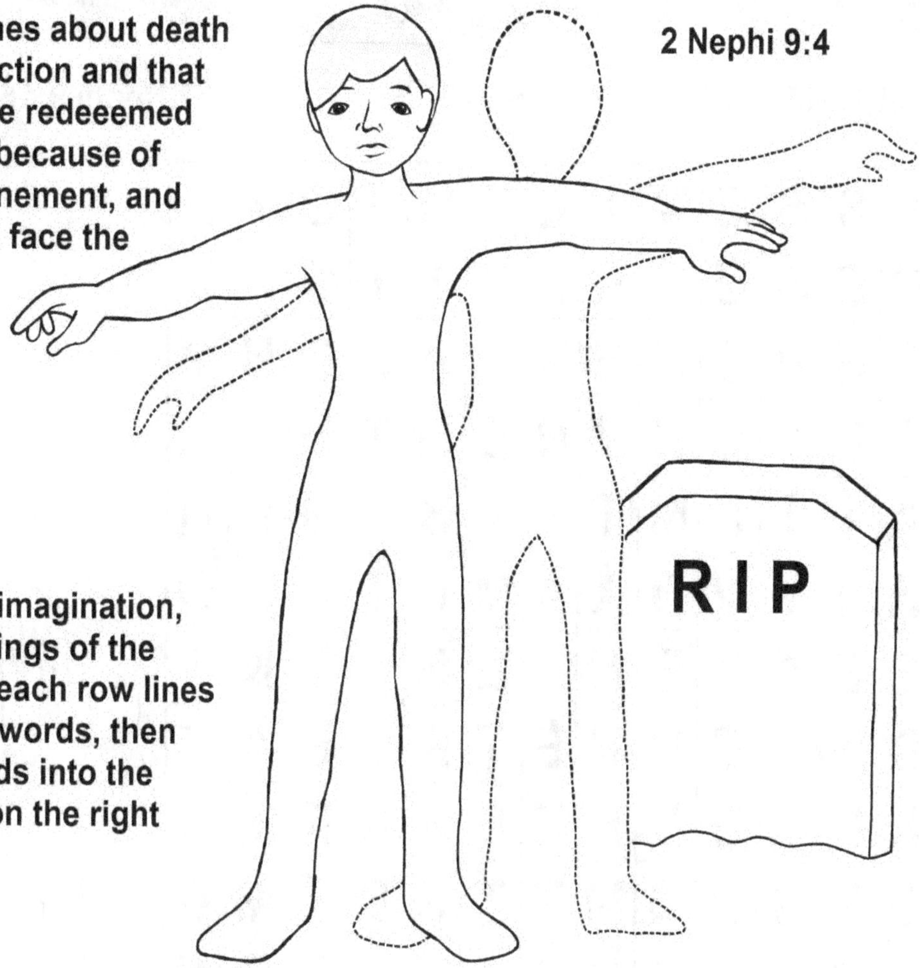

Using your imagination, "spin" the rings of the wheel until each row lines up to make words, then put the words into the sentences on the right side.

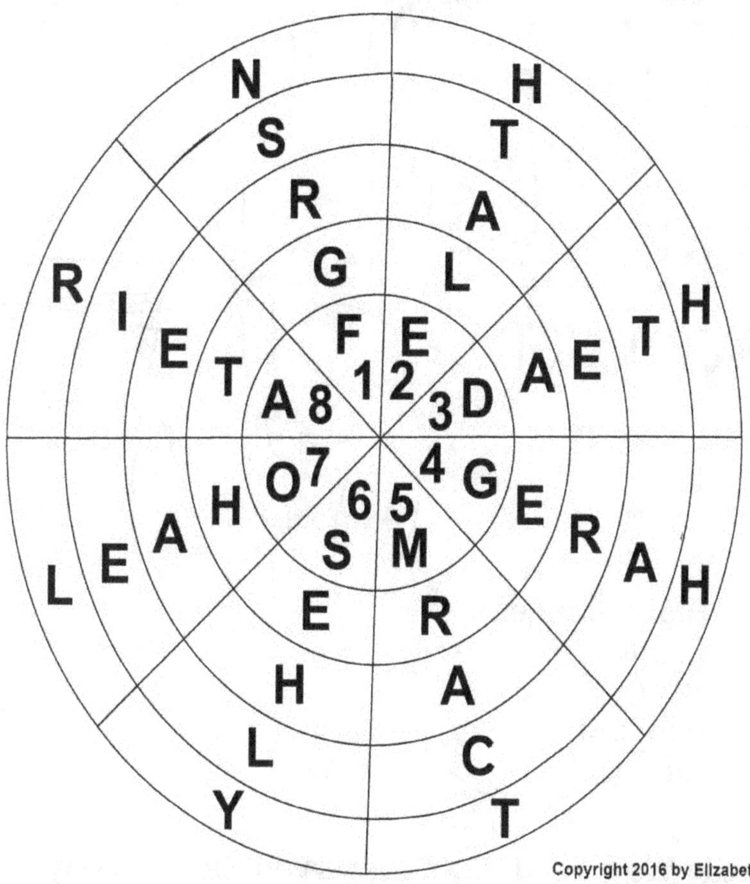

All 1. ________
on 2. ________
suffers
3. ________
but by God's
4. ________
5. ________
we 6. ________
see each
7. ________
8. ________

Day of Judgment

JUDGMENT DAY WORDSEARCH

2 Nephi 9:15

"...then cometh the judgment, and then must they be judged according to the holy judgment of God."

A	L	P	S	S	E	N	I	L	O	H	J	O	Y	E
G	D	R	E	S	U	R	R	E	C	T	I	O	N	E
N	E	E	H	R	E	P	E	N	T	A	S	O	H	M
I	Z	P	L	T	L	N	M	R	E	H	T	N	T	A
T	I	A	I	I	E	M	T	E	I	S	N	U	E	N
S	T	R	V	M	V	D	X	A	M	F	I	H	D	O
A	P	E	E	A	M	E	N	I	E	S	A	T	N	I
L	A	D	T	Y	C	O	R	E	T	R	S	E	A	T
R	B	R	H	U	E	B	R	E	C	P	G	R	M	A
E	R	E	T	S	N	O	M	T	T	S	E	E	M	D
V	N	E	C	I	T	S	U	J	A	H	A	F	O	N
E	T	G	O	D	E	L	L	I	F	L	U	F	C	U
H	T	T	A	E	S	T	N	E	M	G	D	U	J	O
R	I	G	H	T	E	O	U	S	N	E	S	S	●	F

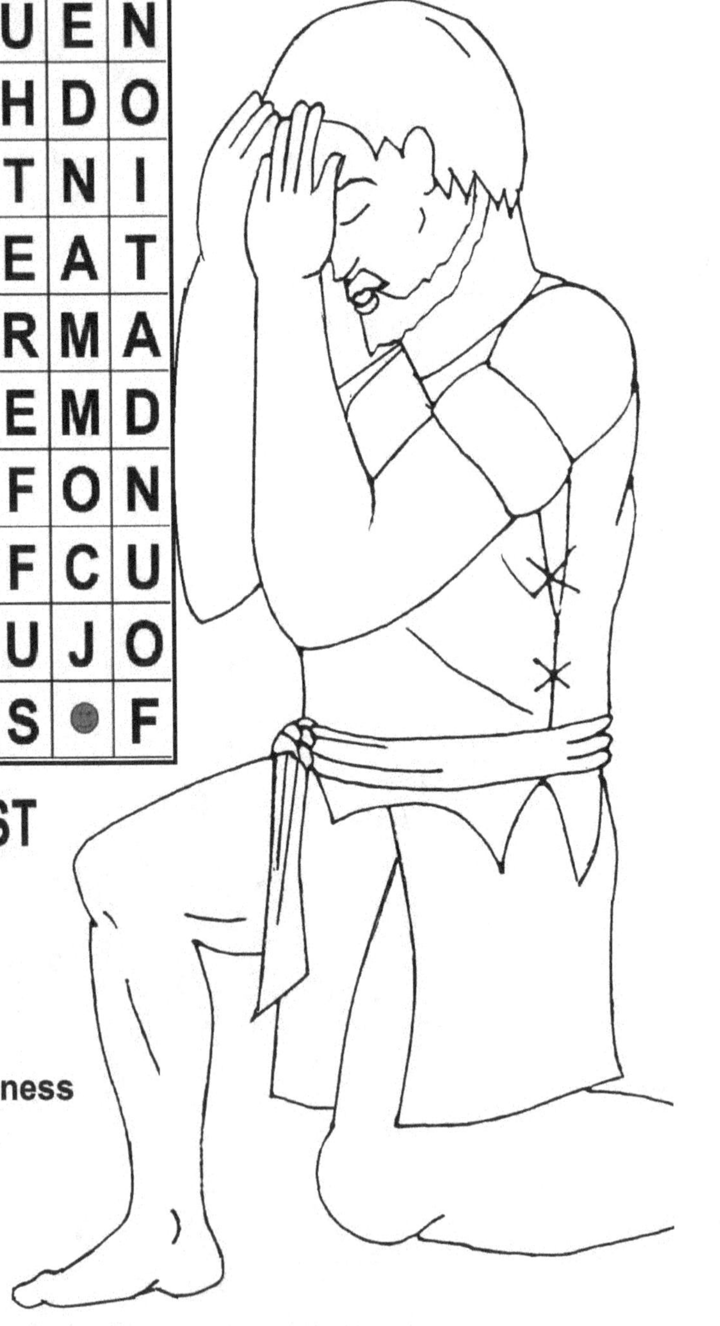

WORD LIST

Ascendeth
Baptized
Brimstone
Commandeth
Delivereth
Everlasting
Executeth
Five
Foundation
Fulfilled
God
Greatness
Hath
Holiness
Immortal
Joy
Justice
Liveth
May
Monster
Name
Prepared
Repent
Resurrection
Righteousness
Saints
Seat
Sendeth
Suffereth

The Atonement Satisfieth

2 Nephi 9:26

The Atonement satisfieth the demands of justice for all those who have not the law given to them.

For the puzzle at right -
When you see the arrow, draw a line to the triangle like this:
When you see a an asterisk, draw a circle around it like this:
When you a diamond, draw a partial circle l like this:

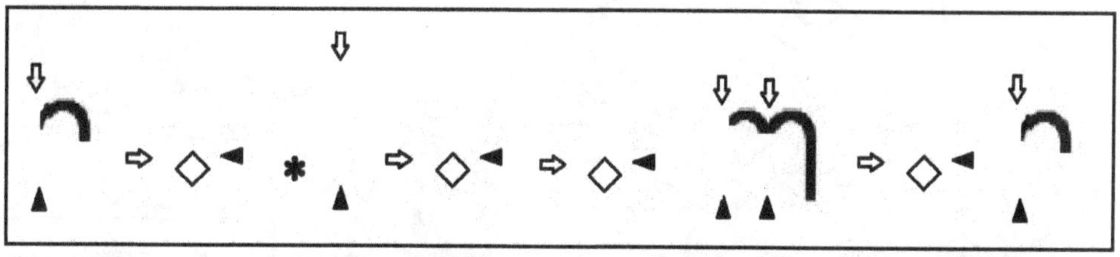

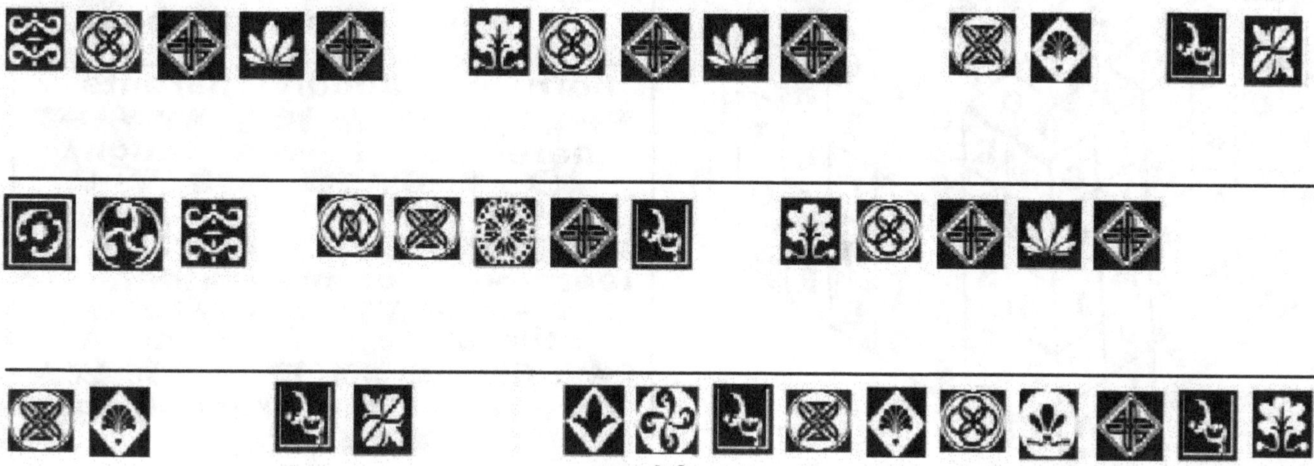

Figure out what the message above says by using the Code Key at right

THIS IS THE CODE KEY

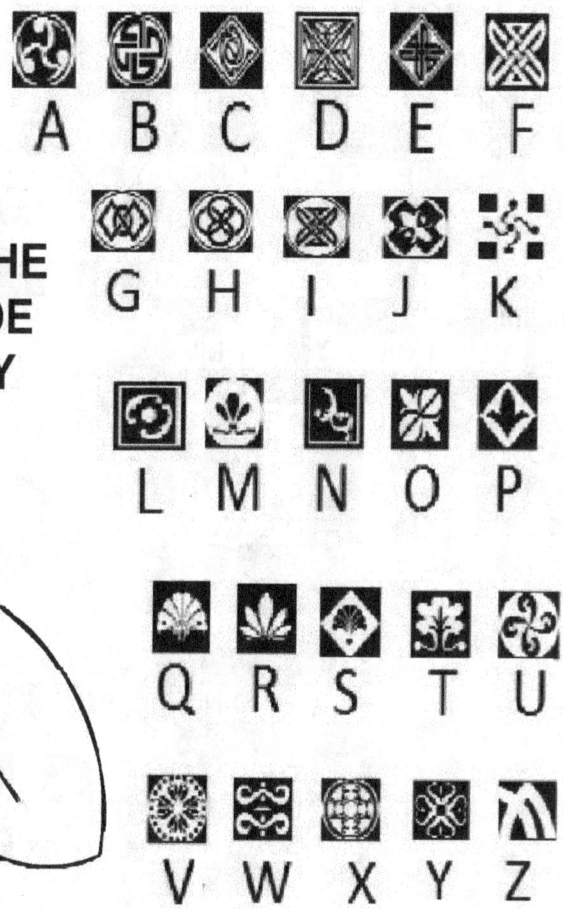

The Book of Mormon Has Been Given Many Names

Title Page

SOLUTION

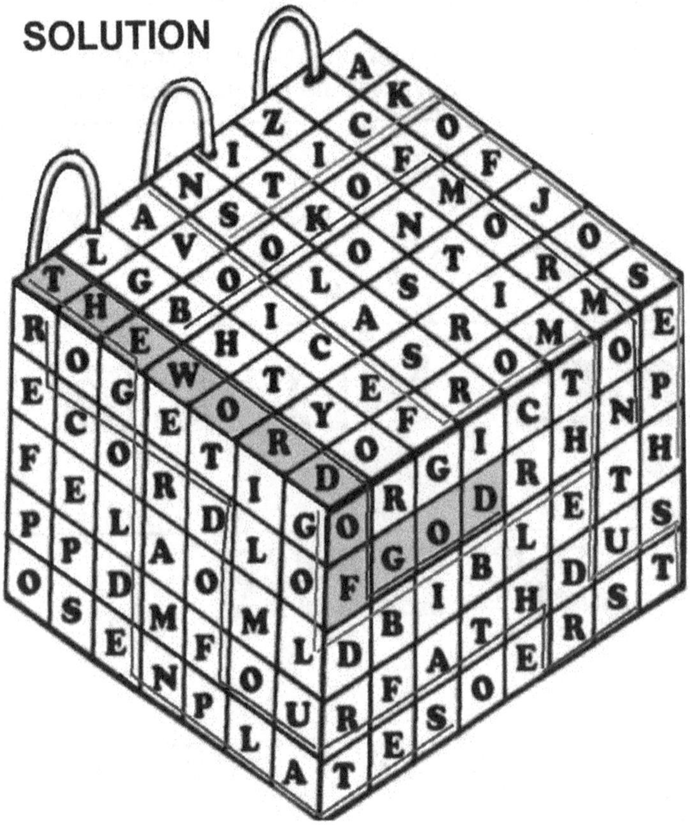

Nephi Made a Record

SOLUTION Page 1

I, Nephi, having been born of goodly parents, therefore I was taught somewhat in all the learning of my father . . . therefore I make a record of my proceedings in my days.

SOLUTION Page 2

LEHI SEES IN A VISION THE DESTRUCTION OF JERUSALEM

LEHI PREACHES TO THE PEOPLE OF JERUSALEM

Page 3

SOLUTION

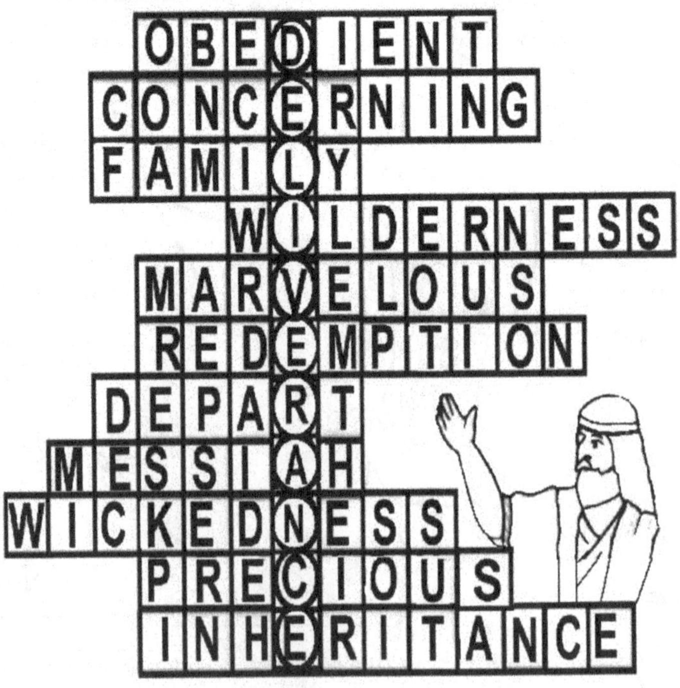

Page 4

Laman and Lemuel Were Unhappy

SOLUTION

M	E	H	T	D	E	T	A	E	R
D	E	H	T	T	O	N	W	E	C
E	U	M	D	I	D	Y	E	N	D
A	R	M	U	R	B	E	H	K	A
L	I	N	G	S	O	C	T	Y	H
					F	A	↑	E	O
					T	U		H	H
					H	S	E	T	W
					A	T	G	O	D

THEY DID MURMUR BECAUSE THEY KNEW NOT THE DEALINGS OF THAT GOD WHO HAD CREATED THEM

Packing Up the Camels

Page 4 B

SOLUTION

Page 5

NEPHI IS DIFFERENT FROM HIS BROTHERS

SOLUTION

YOUNG
OBEDIENT
STRONG
HUMBLE
FAITHFUL
VALIANT

SELFISH
CRUEL
LAZY
WEAK
PROUD

THE JEWS DID MOCK HIM BECAUSE OF THE THINGS WHICH HE TESTIFIED OF THEM AND THEY ALSO SOUGHT HIS LIFE

Page 5b

SOLUTION

Nephi Prays to Understand

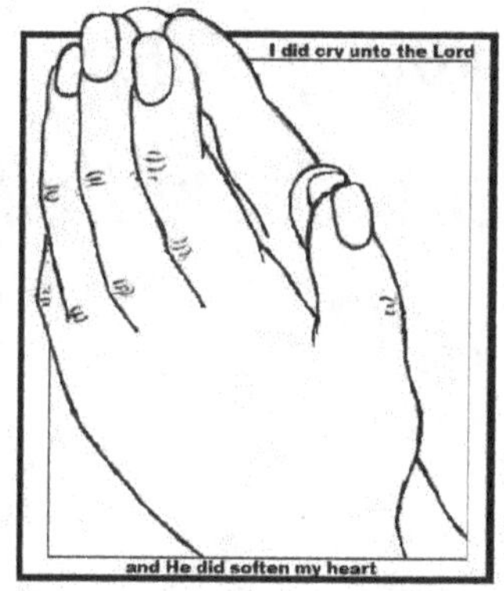

a land I have prepared for you, a land which is choice above all others.

SOLUTION Page 6

I will go and do the things which the Lord hath commanded, for I know the Lord giveth no commandments unto the children of men save he prepareth a way for them that they may accomplish the thing which he commandeth them

Nephi Had Faith

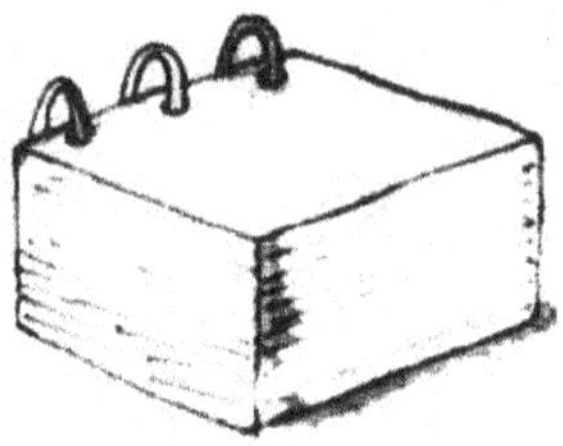

Page 7

Wicked Laban Stole Their Precious Things!

SOLUTION

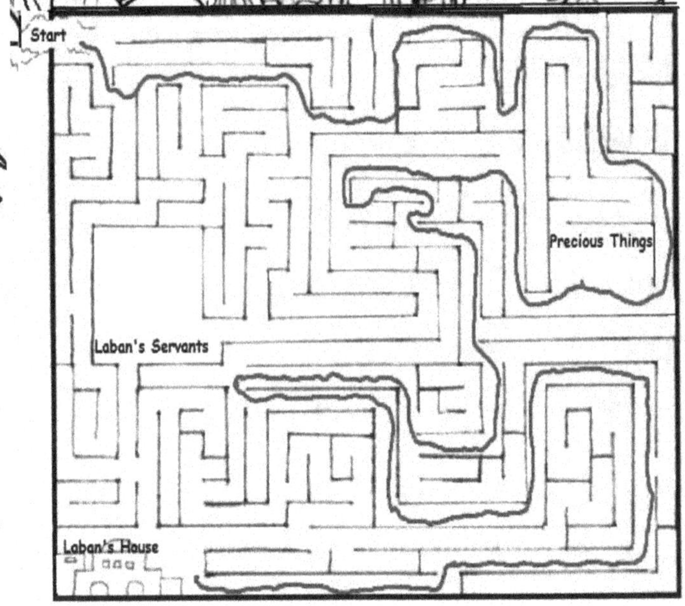

An Angel Appears

Page 7b

SOLUTION

1 *Why do ye smite your younger brother with a rod?*

2 *Know ye not that God hath chosen him to rule over you?*

Page 8

A Record of Great Worth

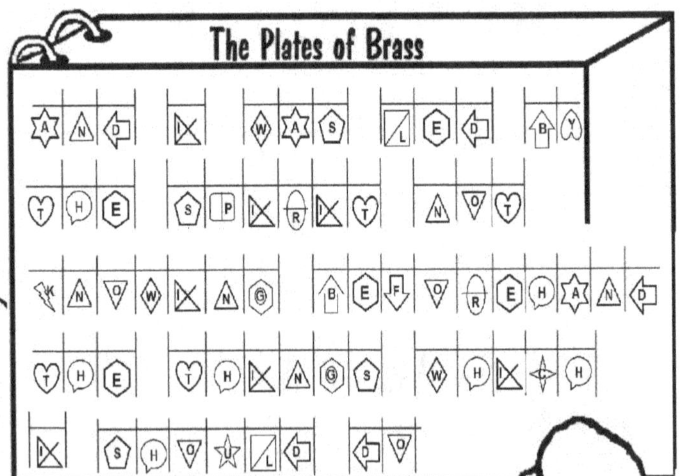

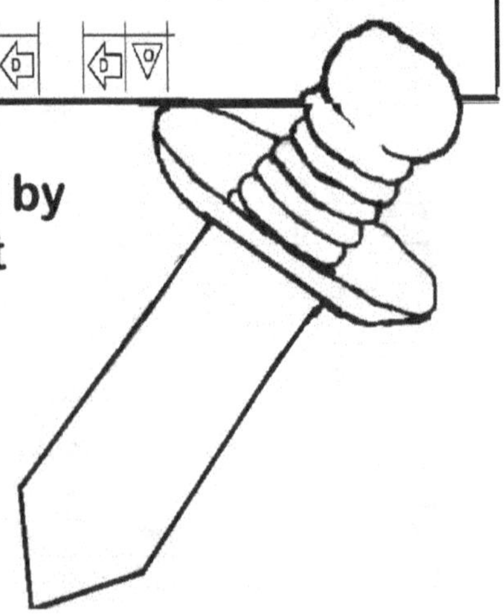

And I was led by the Spirit, not knowing beforehand the things which I should do.

Nephi Convinces Zoram to Join Them

Page 9

SOLUTION

Solution

p.11

PLATES OF GREAT WORTH

The country E G Y P T where Joseph was a slave
Lehi found he was a D E S C E N D A N T of Jose
A man who L A B A N had the brass plates in Jerusalem
The king of Judah in Z E D E K I A H Lehi's time
S A R I A H Nephi's mother
Nephi's oldest brother L A M A N
The ball that L I A H O N A God gave to the Nephites
A N G E L A heavenly messenger
F A M I L Y Father, Mother and children form one

The word on the jumble tower says:

_ _ _ _ _ _ _ _ _ _ _

(Lehi was very happy to have this kind of record of his ancestors!)

Sariah Rejoices

Page 10

SOLUTION

Rebellion

Page 12

Solution

HOW
IS IT
THAT
YE ARE
SO HARD
IN YOUR
HEARTS?

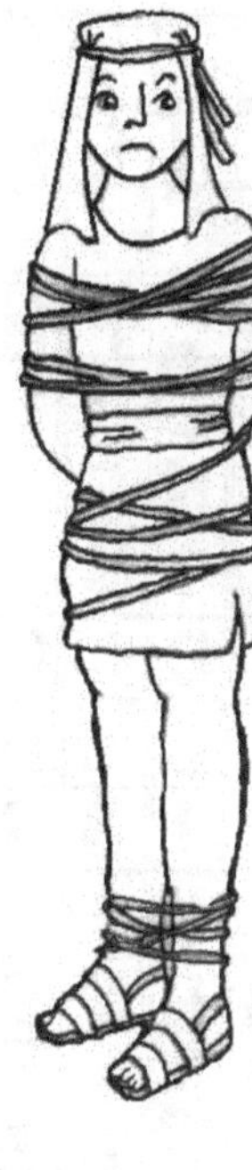

Nephi is Freed!

SOLUTION

Y	E	A		A	N	D		H	O	W			
	I	S		I	T		T	H	A	T			
	Y	E		H	A	V	E		F	O			
R	G	O	T	T	E	N		T	H	A			
T		T	H	E		L	O	R	D				
I	S		A	B	L	E		T	O				
D	O		A	L	L		T	H	I	N			
G	S		A	C	C	O	R	D	I	N			
G		T	O		H	I	S		W	I			
L	L		F	O	R		T	H	E				
C	H	I	L	D	R	E	N		O	F			
M	E	N		I	F		I	T		S			
O		B	E		T	H	A	T		T			
H	E	Y		E	X	E	R	C	I	S			
E		F	A	I	T	H		I	N		H	I	M

Lehi's Vision of the Tree of Life

SOLUTION

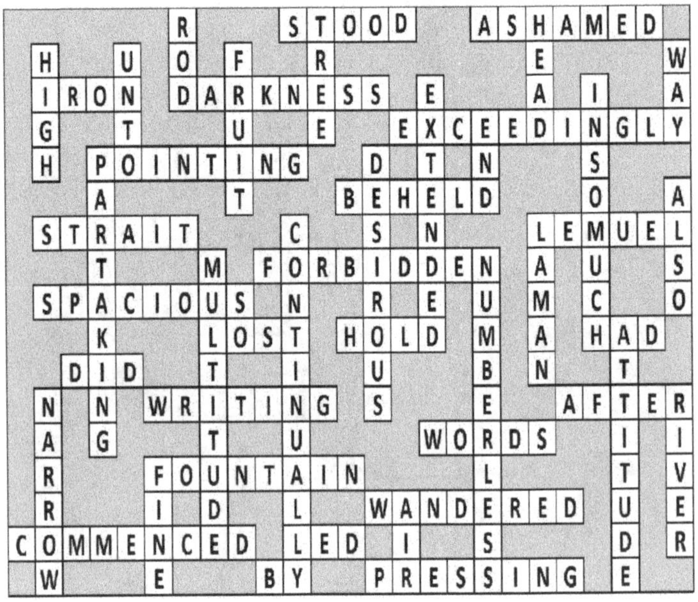

The Tree of Life

SOLUTION

LEHI'S VISION

N	R	O	C	S	P	A	C	I	O	U	S	F	L
T	N	E	R	A	P	E	L	A	M	A	N	I	S
M	I	S	T	R	E	E	O	F	L	I	F	E	E
N	E	P	H	I	H	C	V	P	E	O	P	L	E
P	G	D	E	A	G	I	E	L	U	O	S	D	D
A	N	E	I	H	I	O	O	E	T	E	N	T	L
R	I	M	R	J	H	V	F	U	I	N	I	R	I
T	D	A	O	I	O	H	G	M	U	A	A	A	V
A	L	H	N	C	V	Y	O	E	R	R	T	N	I
K	I	S	R	L	K	E	D	L	F	R	N	O	N
E	U	A	O	I	H	I	R	O	I	O	U	I	G
G	B	M	D	N	'	E	N	D	B	W	O	S	W
R	S	L	I	G	H	T	A	G	N	P	F	I	A
E	S	S	E	N	K	R	A	D	V	A	I	V	T
A	M	A	E	R	D	S	F	I	L	T	H	Y	E
T	I	E	D	U	T	I	T	T	A	H	O	N	R

MAKING PLATES

SOLUTION

E	X	H	O	R	T
23	24	22	42	14	12

P	O	W	E	R
13	42	31	23	14

P	U	R	P	O	S	E
13	44	14	13	42	43	23

R	E	I	G	N
14	23	32	34	51

C	O	M	M	A	N	D	M	E	N	T
54	42	41	41	52	51	11	41	23	51	12

M	U	L	T	I	T	U	D	E
41	44	33	12	32	12	44	11	23

L	O	R	D
33	42	14	11

M	I	N	I	S	T	R	Y
41	32	51	32	43	12	14	53

S	P	E	A	K
43	13	23	52	21

LEHI PROPHESIES OF THE MESSIAH

Page 17

SOLUTION

Clue	Answer	Letter	Scrambled
One long awaited	MESSIAH	(C)	SHEISAMC
One who rescues	SAVIOR	(H)	ORAVISH
One who buys back	REDEEMER	(R)	EMEDERERR
All the people of the earth	MANKIND	(I)	DIMNAKIN
Those who speak for God	PROPHETS	(S)	STREPOPSH
Bear witness or testimony (past tense)	TESTIFIED	(T)	DISTEFETET
The fastener on a shoe (Biblical term)	LATCHET	(I)	LECITATH
Encouraging others to do good	EXHORTING	(A)	THEGOIXNRA
A mission or calling to serve	MINISTRY	(N)	TRININSMY

The Iron Rod

Page 19

SOLUTION

B	E	C	K	O	N	E	D	N	E	V	O	B	A
E	H	G	R	E	A	T	M	I	S	T	F	C	S
M	N	P	A	S	S	H	T	A	P	O	O	F	H
O	A	U	G	H	T	E	S	T	A	N	R	O	A
C	R	T	M	A	N	Y	R	B	C	U	B	U	M
S	R	C	I	B	H	E	S	O	I	D	I	N	E
R	O	D	I	R	E	S	U	T	O	O	D	T	D
E	W	R	I	V	E	R	A	R	U	O	D	A	E
G	O	A	R	N	S	S	L	E	S	T	E	I	K
N	T	W	K	E	T	K	A	E	P	S	N	N	A
I	S	R	S	E	G	N	I	S	S	E	R	P	T
F	A	O	D	R	H	C	U	M	O	S	N	I	R
D	C	F	C	L	I	N	G	I	N	G	O	D	A
E	A	R	T	H	E	X	T	E	N	D	E	D	P

CHRIST

THE OLIVE TREE

Page 18

SOLUTION

Knowest Thou the Meaning of the Tree?

SOLUTION

Page 20

1 Nephi 1:22

The Good Shepherd

For there is one God and one Shepherd over all the earth.

THE GREAT DIVIDE

SOLUTION

V E I L E D
D E V I L
E V I L
L I E
S W A R M S
S W A R M
W A R S
W A S
G R E A S Y
Y E A R S
E A S Y
Y E A
D R O W S E
S W O R D
R O D S
S O D

Twelve Nephite Disciples

SOLUTION

3 Nephi 19:4 is where all the names are listed

Can you figure out which one is which?

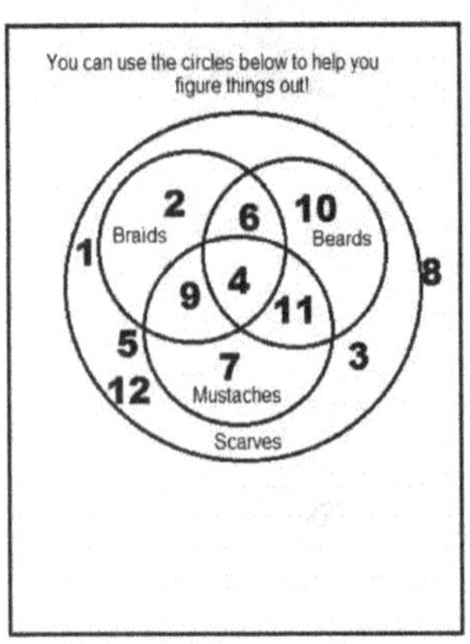

Use these facts to figure out who is who!

Zechariah, Jonas2, Timothy, Mathoni, Nephi, Jeremiah and Shemnon all have braids.

Isaiah, Jonas1, Mathoni, Jonas2, and Jeremiah all have beards.

Nephi, Mathoni, Kumen, Timothy, and Kumenonhi all are wearing head scarves.

Jonas1, Timothy, Jonas2, Isaiah, Mathoniahah, Kumen, Mathoni and Shemnon all have mustaches.

Who is Who?

1. **Nephi**
2. **Zechariah**
3. **Mathoni**
4. **Jonas2**
5. **Timothy**
6. **Jeremiah**
7. **Mathonihah**
8. **Kumenonhi**
9. **Shemnon**
10. **Isaiah**
11. **Jonas1**
12. **Kumen**

And He Went Forth Upon the Many Waters

SOLUTION

vision of the abominable C H U R C H
and T H E vision of the
T R E E of Life
N E P H I
S A W that
the G E N T I L E S
came O U T of captivity
and these P E O P L E
were W H I T E and fair
like unto his own P E O P L E
B E F O R E they were slain.

And they C A M E forth
and did P R O S P E R
in the L A N D
The Spirit W R O U G H T upon them
to come to the P R O M I S E D land
because they were H U M B L E
The wrath of God was U N T O all those
who fought A G A I N S T them.

A Record of the Jews via the Gentiles

Page 25

SOLUTION

T	H	E	■	P	L	A	I	N	■	A	N	D	■	P	R	E	C	I	O	U	S
T	H	I	N	G	S	■	W	H	I	C	H	■	H	A	V	E	■	B	E	E	N
T	A	K	E	N	■	A	W	A	Y	■	F	R	O	M	■	T	H	E	M	■	■
T	H	K	N	N	S	A	W	N	Y	C	F	D	H	M	V	T	C	B	O	U	N
T	A	E	E	P	L	A	I	A	I	A	N	R	O	A	R	E	H	E	M	E	S
T	H	I		G			W	H			H			P		E		I	E		

For There Shall be... One Shepherd Over All the Earth

Page 27 Solution

AND THE TIME COMETH THAT HE SHALL MANIFEST HIMSELF UNTO ALL NATIONS

These Things Shall Come Forth Unto Thy Seed

Page 26

SOLUTION

An
A N G E L
S P A K E
with
A W F U L
P O W E R

to

B R I N G
F O R T H
P L A I N
T R U T H

There are Save Two Churches Only

Page 28

SOLUTION

For the time cometh saith the Lamb of God that I will work a great and a marvelous work among the children of men: a work which shall be everlasting, either on the one hand or the other – either to the convincing of them unto peace and life eternal, or unto the deliverance of them to the hardness of their hearts and the blindness of their minds unto their being brought down into captivity, and also into destruction, both temporally and spiritually according to the captivity of the devil.

Page 29

He Shall Write Concerning the End of the World

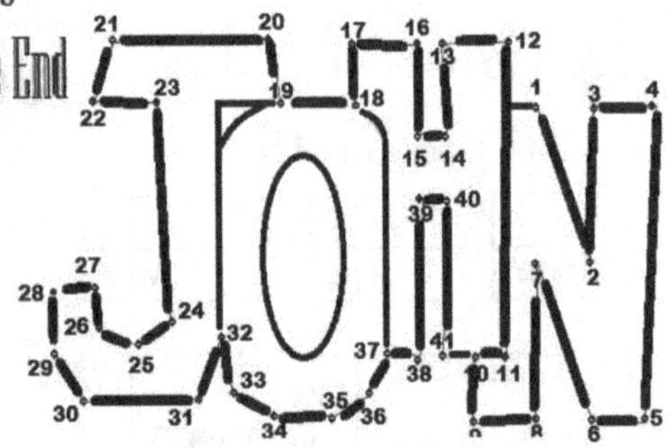

SOLUTION

4	7	10	6	9	12				
B	E	H	O	L	D				
6	8	7		6	3		5	10	
O	N	E		O	F		T	H	E
5	8	7	9	8	7				
T	W	E	L	V	E				
11	4	6	8	5	9	7	8		
A	P	O	S	T	L	E	S		
6	3		5	10	7				
O	F		T	H	E				
9	11	1	4						
L	A	M	B						

Nephi Prays for Knowledge

Page 30 Solution

Because of the HARDNESS of their hearts, when Nephi's brothers LEARNED of the teachings, they did not UNDERSTAND.

Unlike his BROTHERS, Nephi was OVERCOME by grief BECAUSE of what he had see in vision CONCERNING his seed. His brothers DISPUTED among themselves.

Nephi asked them, "Have ye INQUIRED of the Lord?

Then he explained how Lehi had SPOKEN of the Jews (the olive tree) as the NATURAL branches and the Gentiles as those who were grafted in.

But Nephi was still sorrowful because he had foreseen the DESTRUCTION of all his seed (descendants.)

He Shall Write

Page 29b SOLUTION

B/R	A/E	H/C	K/O	L/T	D/K	I/H	Y/E	P/S
I/H	F/A	E/L	L/D	S/F	K/E	Y/E	O/A	U/N
D/B	W/T	R/M	E/I	T/S	I/E	M/S	S/A	O/N
I/Y	T/S	H/P	Y/I	N/U	A/G	S/F	W/P	O/H
E/I	C/W	H/P	H/M	K/A	E/V	G/E	A/B	Y/E
							O/E	N/U

Cross out all the vowels that are on the top half
Cross out all these letters F J K P Q U
Cross out all the B C D M R T W that are on the bottom except B in row 5
Cross out S on the bottom except on row 1 and all S on row 3
Cross out GVY on the top half
The remaining letters have a message

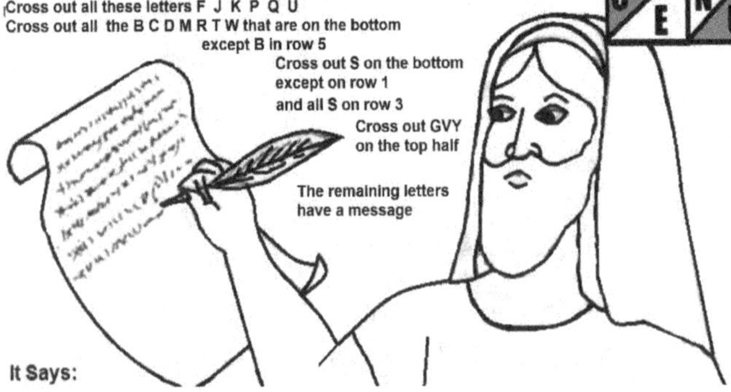

It Says:

Behold, he shall see and write many things which have been

A Branch of Israel

Page 31 SOLUTION

THE

REMNANT OF OUR SEED SHALL KNOW THAT THEY ARE OF THE HOUSE OF ISRAEL

Nephi's Brothers ask him about the Tree of Life

Page 32

SOLUTION

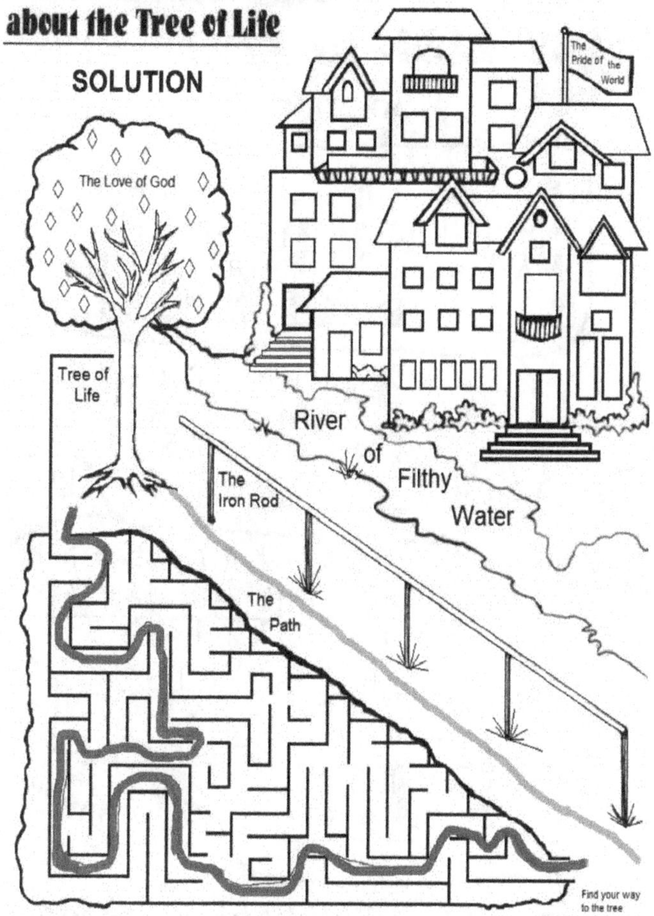

SOLUTION Page 34

Nephi Exhorts His Brethren

Page 33

T / A	W / H	F / E	G / U	U / L	
G / I	L / R	T / E	A / Y	T / T	
A / D	E / K	E / U	T / I	L / H	
T / D	W / H	E / E	T / L	R / L	
U / T	R / T	H / U	T / T	H / O	
S / B	E / P	O / H	A / K	R / E	N / D

1. A W F U L
2. G R E A T
3. D E V I L
4. D W E L L
5. T R U T H
6. S P O K E N

SOLUTION

THE GUILTY TAKETH THE TRUTH TO BE HARD

Finding Game SOLUTION

Page 35

Camel Travel SOLUTION

Page 36

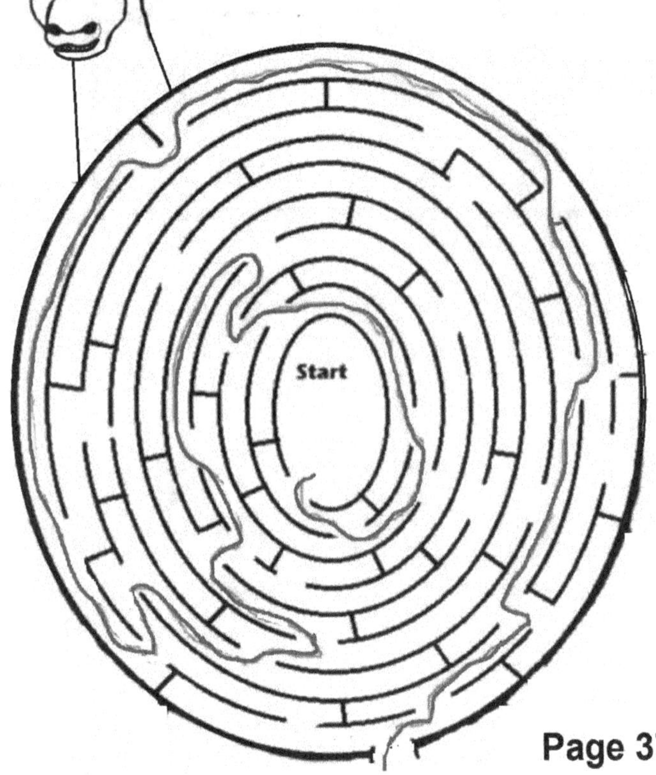

NEPHI'S BROTHERS WERE VERY RUDE TO HIM!

Page 38

Solution

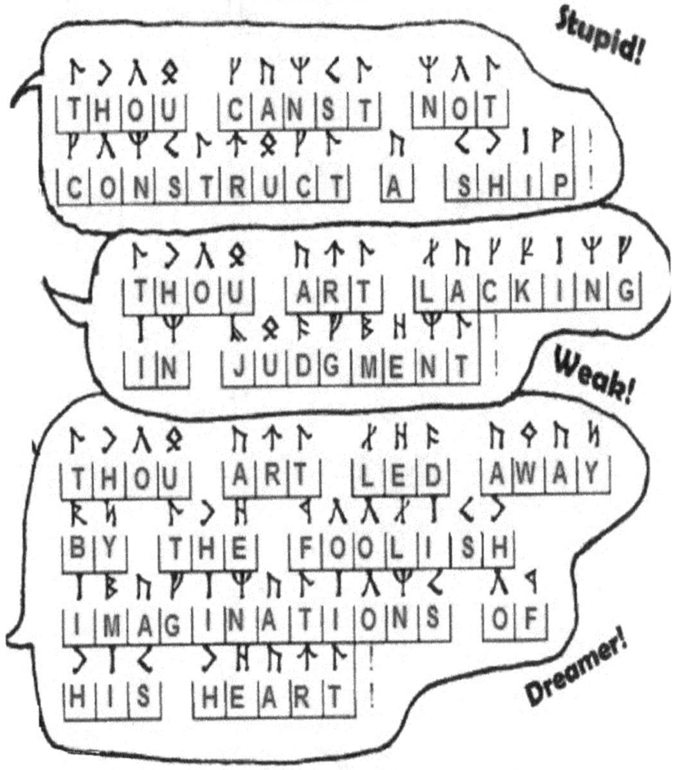

Page 37

Building the Ship

SOLUTION

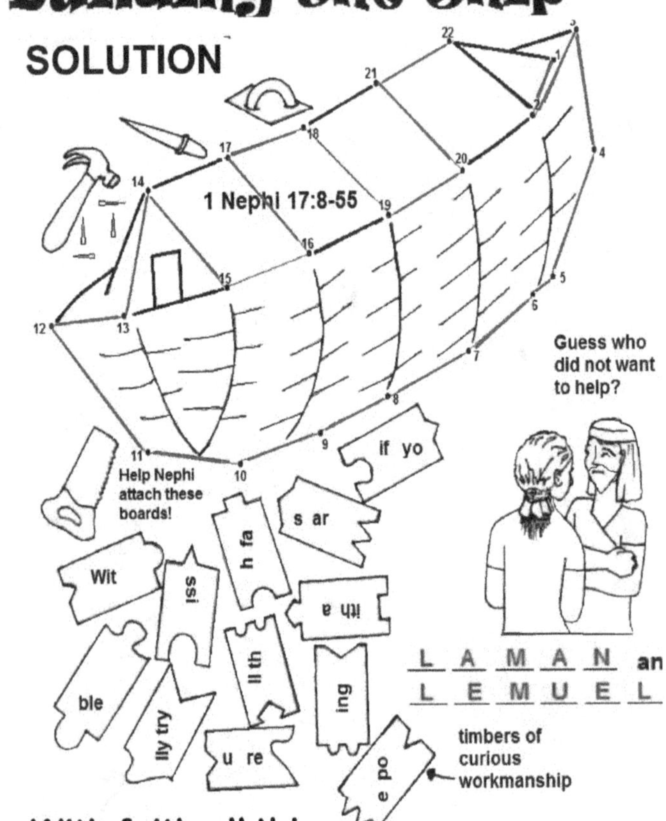

With faith all things are possible if you really try

God's Lovely Creation

Solution

Page 39

Behold, the Lord hath created the earth that it should be inhabited and he hath created his children that they should possess it

1 Beh	2 old,	3 ...th	4 e...L
5 ord	6 ....ha	7 th...	8 cre
9 ate	10 d...t	11 he...	12 ear
13 th...	14 tha	15 t...i	16 t...s
17 ho	18 uld	19 ...be	20 ....in
21 hab	22 ite	23 d;...	24 ...an
25 d...h	26 e...h	27 ath	28 ...cr
29 eat	30 ed...	31 his	32 ...ch
33 ild	34 ren	35 ...th	36 at...
37 th...	38 ey...	39 sho	40 uld
41 ...po	42 sse	43 ss...	44 ...it.

Touch Me Not! Solution Page 40

THE POWER OF GOD

T	R	R	E	M	E	M	B	E	R	N	A	M	E
D	E	D	N	A	M	M	O	C	D	L	I	U	B
T	H	G	U	A	N	H	D	E	E	R	L	R	H
U	T	P	D	O	G	G	Y	E	P	E	E	M	E
B	I	H	E	U	P	O	U	A	T	D	G	U	D
S	W	T	O	R	R	M	S	I	H	N	N	R	I
U	O	R	O	T	I	U	U	W	S	U	A	M	V
O	U	A	S	I	N	S	C	F	R	H	D	U	I
R	L	E	E	D	I	T	H	E	S	T	E	R	D
I	D	F	E	R	Q	R	E	E	O	H	N	D	H
S	F	R	P	E	U	C	L	L	D	E	I	E	G
E	K	I	L	W	I	F	A	I	E	M	A	R	F
D	H	C	U	O	T	O	N	N	O	R	P	S	E
S	E	A	V	P	Y	D	D	G	T	H	R	O	W

Sailing to the Promised Land Page 41b

SOLUTION

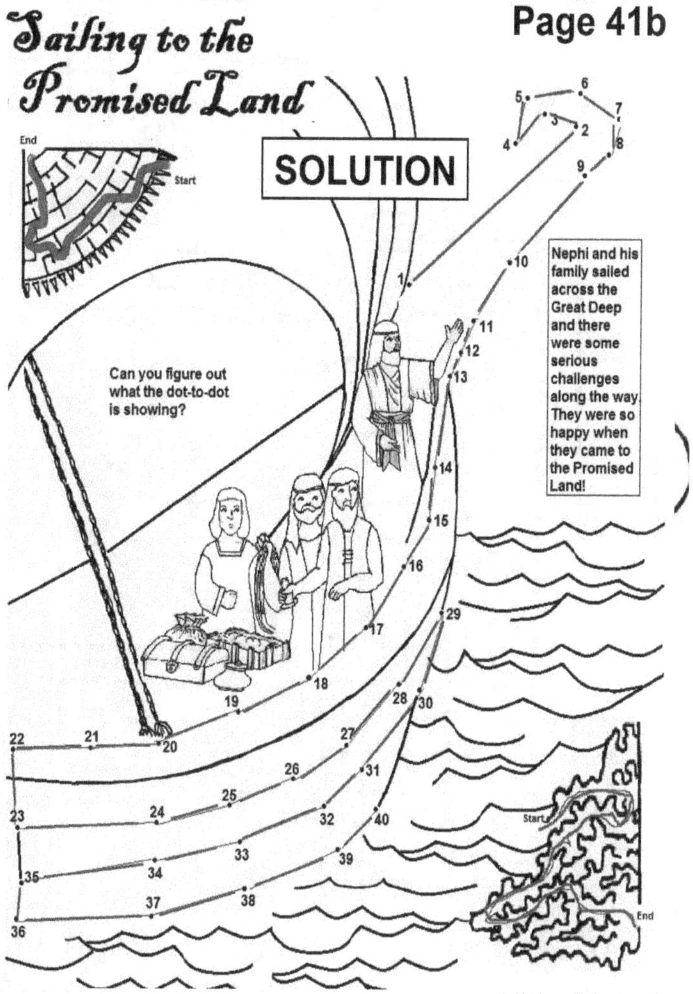

SOLUTION Page 41

Nephi Builds a Ship

Put each board of the ship into the right place to see what the message says:

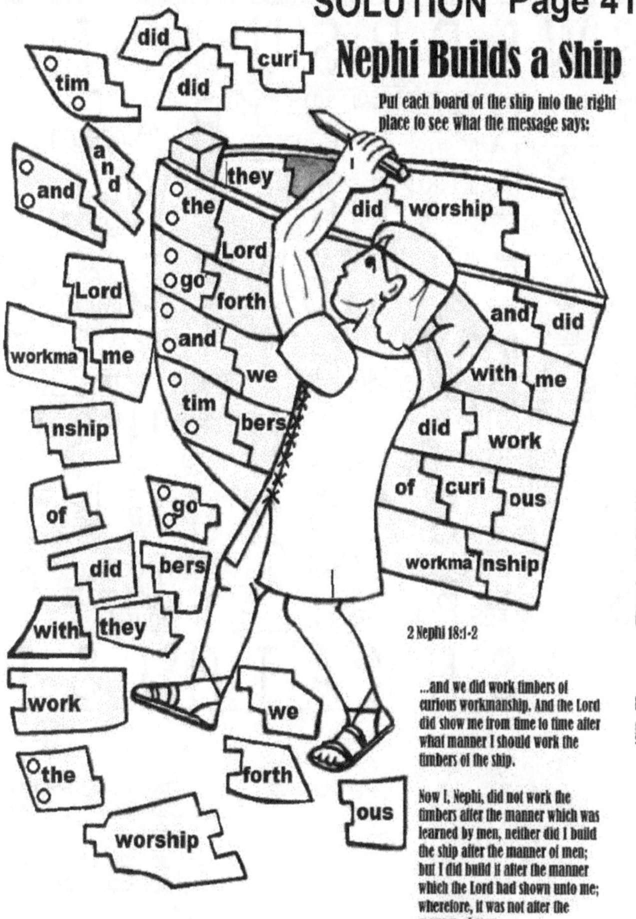

2 Nephi 18:1-2

...and we did work timbers of curious workmanship. And the Lord did show me from time to time after what manner I should work the timbers of the ship.

Now I, Nephi, did not work the timbers after the manner which was learned by men, neither did I build the ship after the manner of men; but I did build it after the manner which the Lord had shown unto me; wherefore, it was not after the manner of men.

A Bad Storm Page 42

Solution

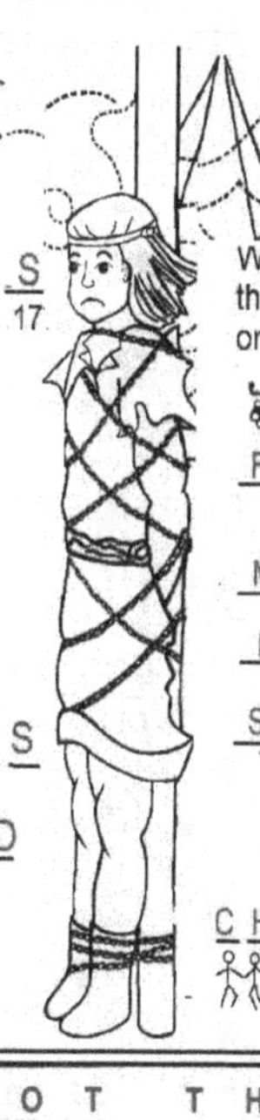

T I M B E R S
16 27 26 36 19

s) P R O V I S I O N S
28 14 35 29 17

C O M P A S S
7 18

T E M P E S T
2 32 1

sual) C U R I O U S
40 6 10 20

F I N I S H E D
15 4 9

A F F L I C T I O N S
3 8 4 22

F R I G H T E N E D
34 11 33 41 5 21 25 31

ater) D R O W N E D
23 24 30 13 12

What did they take on the ship?

F R U I T S

M E A T

H O N E Y

S E E D S

W I V E S

C H I L D R E N

W E W I L L N O T T H A T
30 1 30 15 8 8 13 14 5 2 4 3 16

1 Nephi 18:6

O U R Y O U N G E R B R O T H E R
29 40 23 7 20 25 33 12 6 27 11 24 2 4 21 28

S H A L L B E A R U L E R
17 41 18 8 8 27 9 3 36 40 8 32 23

O V E R U S
22 35 31 36 20 19

(This is what his elder brothers said about Nephi)

BOOK OF MORMON ANIMALS Page 43

SOLUTION

Solution

Page 45

E	R	S
T	■	Q
R	A	U

S	S	E
D	■	N
A	R	K

I	E	L
Y	■	D
H	T	E

R	R	E
E	■	B
M	E	M

P	I	S
S	■	E
E	D	D

C	S	D
O	■	E
U	R	G

Answers:
Remember
Despised
Scourged
Quarters
Darkness
Yieldeth

Can you figure out these words from this page? They go in a circle and can go either way.

I Had Made These Plates... Solution Page 44

```
I H W T H T T R A N S P I R E D K A E P S N I A L P
G U E H P S N O I T C U R T S N I A E S I W O U L D
E N A E C P O A F S H D S M I T E C E R O F E B C D
N D K Y B O T H E O S O C M D R O C E R U O A H D S
E R N E M K M E E U E G O T H P R O P H E C I E S S
R E E S T E E M T L L J U D G E E U S H A L L N E E
A D S O N N W I A G F E R R W H E N A R D S O E G S
T D S T L R P N D N L K G H T U R T Y R O I J R A S
I L I A I D T I L I D A E N W O N K E E T E E G D O
O O O T H E R S R K E M Y S E L F N S C N L R I N P
N H E B L E F T O A Y S E S W W A E U I U P U V O C
D E V I E C E R W M R C A N A Y O R O O M M S E B O
H B T N F O G Y C A I C B O T V T R M U N A A S F U
A U X I S R Y S W O R G O N E S E M T S A R L D A N
V T A Q M P P I V E N H D D E E R E W H U T E R T S
E X C U S E T H D N W A Y D G N I V O L G M M A H E
S N O I T N E T N O C R N M O R F U R T H E R W E L
P A R T S U P O N D E A N G E L C O M E T H E O R S
N A E Y E A R S T V L S E T A L P H E R E A F T E R
```

I HAD MADE THESE PLATES BY WAY OF COMMANDMENT

Liken the Scriptures Unto Us Page 46 SOLUTION

hopes posse south
sneek saved spoof
other paper stash
stoke thank

brass Jacob Moses spake truth
every Judah mouth speak weary
forth lands needs swear which
hosts liken sinew teach words
house might smite those would

Peace Like A River

SOLUTION

O that thou hadst hearkened to my commandments - then had thy peace been as a river, thy righteousness as the waves of the sea. 1 Nephi 20: 19

Nephi Quotes Isaiah

SOLUTION

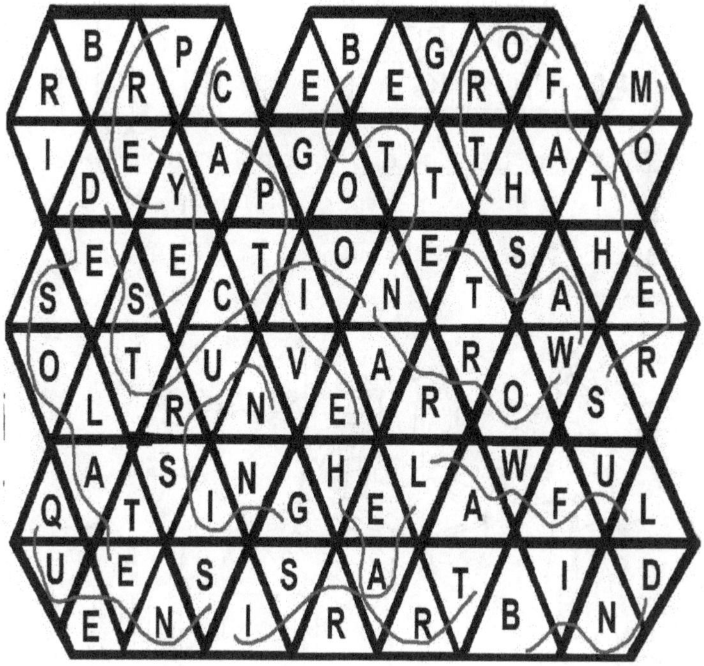

the prophet isaiah

1 Nephi 21

SOLUTION

Can you fit all the four letter words into the puzzle?

Four-by-Four

ALSO	MADE
DAYS	NAME
DONE	ROCK
ENDS	SAID
EVEN	SAVE
EYES	SHOW
FEED	THAT
FLOW	THEE
FREE	THEM
FROM	THEY
GIVE	THIS
HAND	THOU
HATH	THUS
HAVE	TIME
HEAT	UNTO
HIGH	VAIN
HOLY	WAYS
LAST	WHOM
LEAD	WILL
LIKE	WITH
LIVE	WOMB
LORD	WORK

Scattered Israel

1 Nephi 22:3

SOLUTION

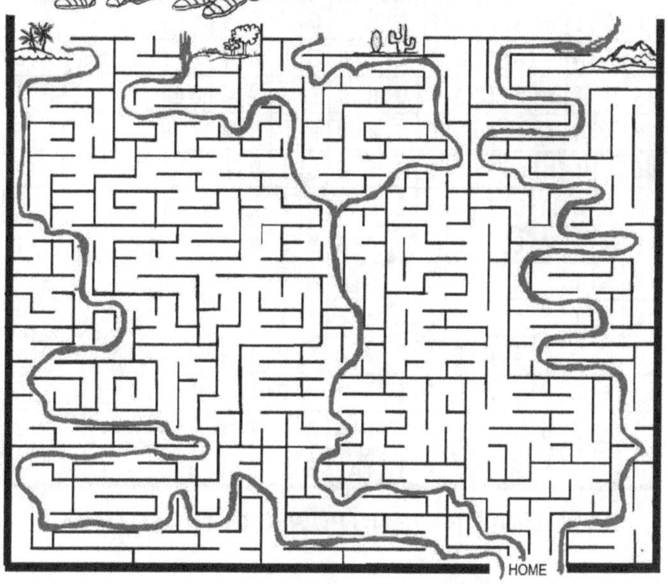

In the Latter Days

SOLUTION

WIL	ELO	A M
ARV	WOR	ROC
G T	HE	MON
US	L P	DO
EED	TO	K A

GOD W I L L P R O C E E D T O D O

A M A R V E L O U S W O R K

A M O N G T H E GENTILES

Fill the blanks with the word sections in the squares above to see what it says.

1 Nephi 22: 51

Jerusalem is Destroyed!

SOLUTION

I		H	A	V	E		S	E	E	N		A
R5		L7	L8	L9	L3		R8	L8	L0	L4		L5

V	I	S	I	O	N		I	N		W	H	I	C	H
L9	R3	R2	L2	L4	L6		L11	R11		L3	R6	R7	R1	L8

I		K	N	O	W		T	H	A	T
R7		L1	L9	R6	L9		L10	L5	L8	L8

J	E	R	U	S	A	L	E	M		I	S
L6	R2	L3	R4	R7	R4	R1	R8	R9		L3	R2

D	E	S	T	R	O	Y	E	D
R2	R11	R8	L4	L7	R5	L7	R5	R10

FUTURE DAYS

SOLUTION

R	E	W	H	A	T	S	O	E	V	E	R	M	O	D	G	N	I	K	N	O	W
E	E	X	S	S	D	H	P	H	A	F	T	D	E	D	N	U	O	F	N	O	C
S	R	W	E	R	S	E	R	T	R	F	O	L	D	N	E	R	D	L	I	H	C
T	A	A	O	C	Q	A	O	E	M	I	T	U	S	E	V	L	A	C	N	N	R
A	L	W	O	P	U	R	P	R	B	N	G	W	R	P	Y	D	O	F	F	E	E
B	C	M	W	G	A	T	H	E	R	E	T	H	I	H	F	E	E	D	L	D	F
L	E	L	H	N	R	S	E	B	E	S	O	H	T	I	A	S	S	F	P	R	F
I	D	H	O	A	T	U	T	M	T	H	U	S	G	E	S	T	O	O	V	A	U
S	W	I	C	K	E	D	L	U	H	D	E	E	N	I	O	R	P	E	E	H	S
H	Z	N	F	I	R	E	O	N	R	U	P	O	N	W	F	U	L	N	E	S	S
E	E	I	N	A	S	M	O	K	E	E	O	I	D	R	L	C	S	C	U	T	P
D	P	Q	M	O	C	W	S	E	N	R	A	E	F	A	T	T	B	N	S	S	E
L	M	U	U	E	K	E	E	R	A	G	V	S	R	T	R	I	E	U	E	I	R
R	A	I	S	A	V	E	D	P	D	R	N	A	B	H	E	O	L	S	N	S	I
O	N	T	T	A	K	O	E	N	E	E	T	Y	U	S	M	N	O	T	E	H	S
W	N	Y	P	A	O	E	O	S	V	O	S	H	I	E	B	M	N	E	M	D	H
I	E	O	P	L	I	K	E	E	I	W	R	O	L	L	L	S	G	N	I	H	T
L	R	S	B	I	S	R	A	E	L	A	A	L	T	F	E	N	G	I	E	R	A
L	A	E	R	A	P	E	R	P	Y	S	R	Y	E	L	B	B	U	T	S	I	H

SATAN WILL HAVE NO POWER IN THOSE DAYS

Lehi Counsels His Children

SOLUTION

HIDDEN PICTURES - Can you find: duck, fish, mouse, turtle, seahorse, rabbit, 2 sheep, 2 birds, 3 snakes, tooth axe, broom, bell, knife, fork, spoon, horn, jingle bell, cowry shell, sailboat, 2 keys

2 Nephi 1:7

Lehi tells his children that this land is consecrated to those he brings to dwell in it, and if they will serve him and keep his commandments they will be blessed, and prospered and it will be a land of liberty to them, but if they do not, they will eventually be swept off.

Shake Off Those Chains! Page 55

SOLUTION

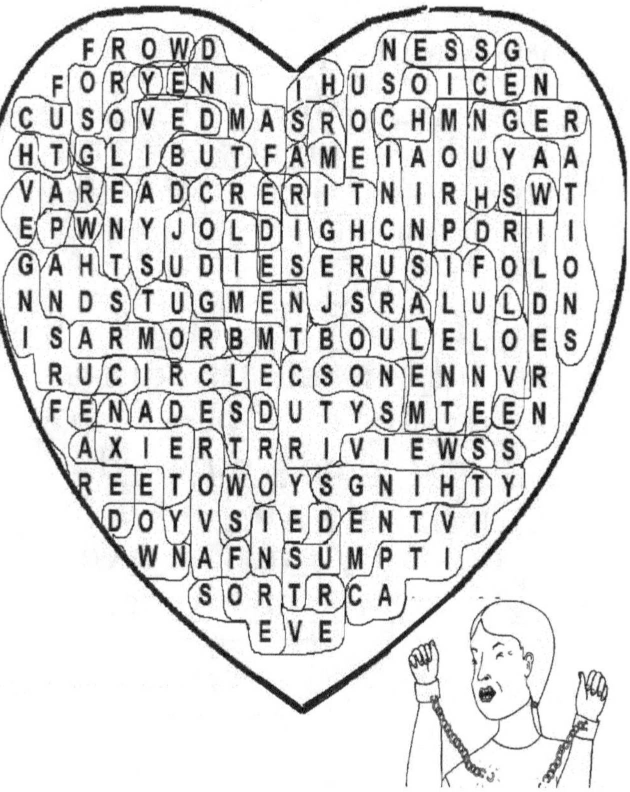

The Light of Christ Page 57

SOLUTION

Page 56

SOLUTION

ANGRY BROTHERS

Laman and Lemuel accuse Nephi of seeking for power and...

Follow the paths to put the letters in the right order

SOLUTION Page 58

Opposition In All Things

F	J	M	W	G	K	F	H	I	T	S	H	U
T	U	V	E	X	Z	R	Q	W	D	U	B	Y
L	K	G	T	D	O	K	U	F	V	T	Z	X
B	E	Z	S	J	T	F	C	Z	W	G	O	V
V	B	M	D	T	W	P	U	X	T	J	K	A
D	G	X	T	Q	N	G	F	D	G	Y	Z	F

Cross out all of the following letters in the paragraph above and you will find a message:

B D F G H J K Q T U V W Y Z

MISERY LOVES COMPANY

The Purpose of Life

Page 59

SOLUTION

Two Sticks

Page 61

SOLUTION

Wherefore the fruit of thy loins shall write; and the fruit of the loins of Judah shall write; and that which shall be written shall grow together unto the confounding of false doctrines and laying down of contentions.

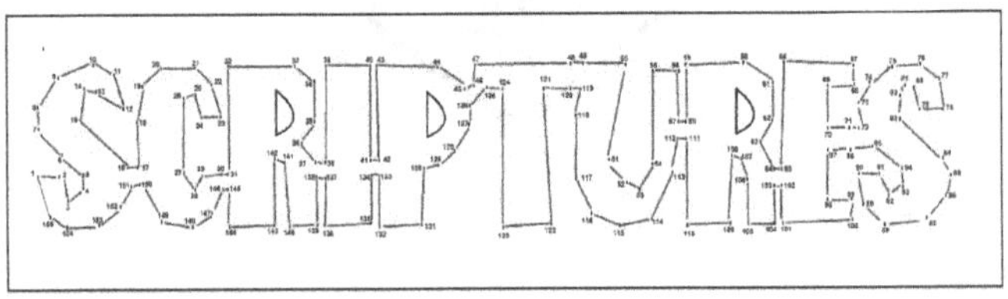

Joseph and Joseph

P. 60

SOLUTION

A Promise to the Lamanites

Page 62

SOLUTION

THERE SHALL RISE UP ONE
MIGHTY AMONG THEM WHO
SHALL DO MUCH GOOD...UNTO
THE SEED OF THY BRETHREN

Nephi Loves...

SOLUTION

1. My God hath been my support; he hath led me through mine afflictions in the wilderness.

2. And upon these I write the things of my soul and many of the scriptures...

M A Y N G D O U D P H O A N T T H H B E E S E E
N I M W Y R S I U T P E P T O H R E T T H H E I
H N A G T S H O L F E M D Y M S E O T U H L R A
O N U D G M H A M N I Y N O E F A T F H F E L S
I C C R T I I P O T N U S R I E N S - the wilderness

LAMANITES AND NEPHITES

SOLUTION

- ● color yellow or orange
- ●● color gray or brown
- ●●● color red
- x color blue

If you only have a pencil:
light gray
medium gray
dark gray
black

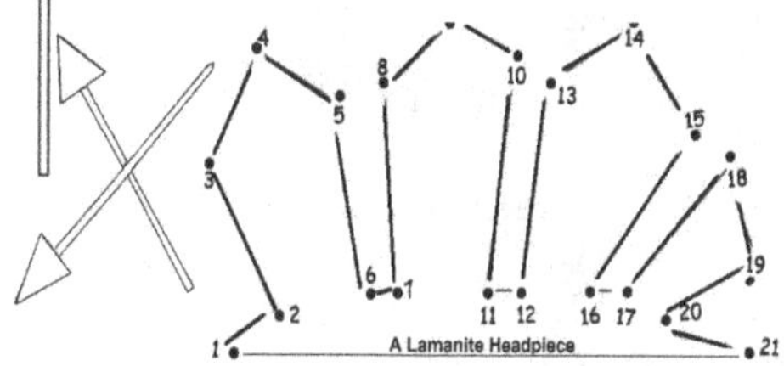

A Lamanite Headpiece

The Psalm of Nephi SOLUTION

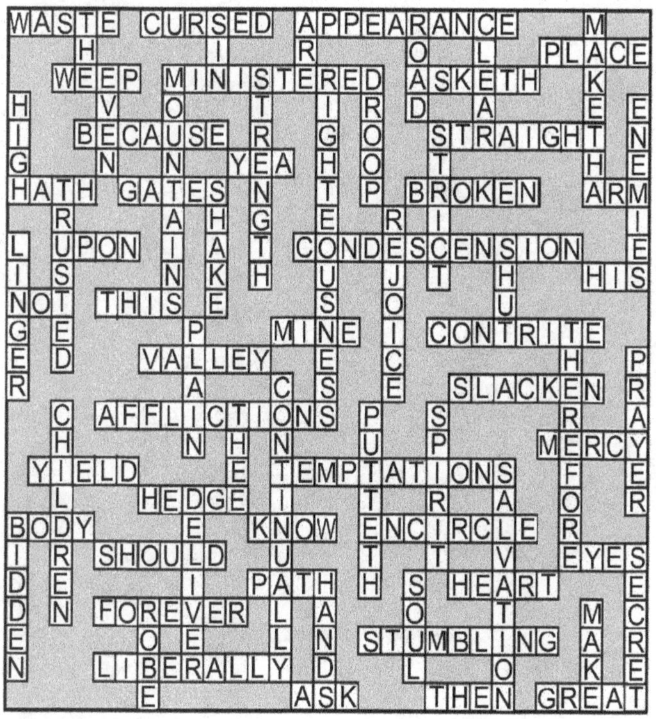

The Nephites Prosper

SOLUTION

And I did teach my people to build buildings and to work in all manner of wood and of iron and of copper and of brass and of steel and of gold and of silver and of precious ores.

And I Nephi, did build a temple...

Draw your own house here:

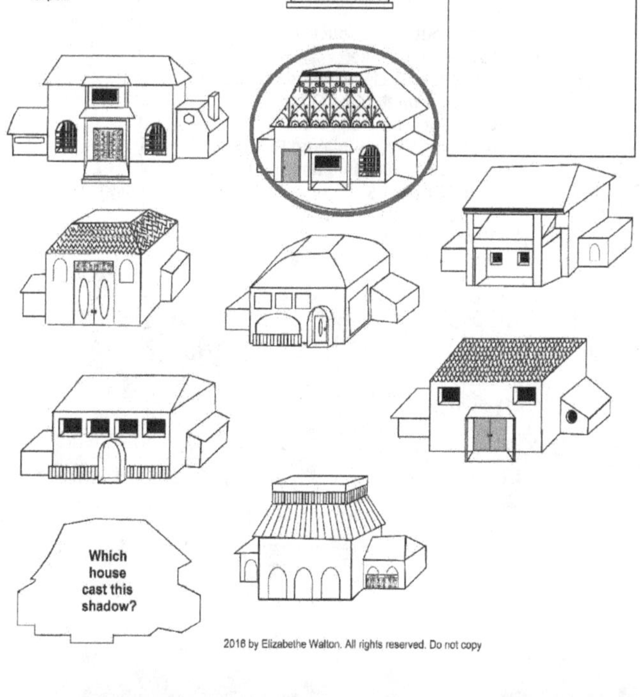

Consecrated Brothers

Page 67

SOLUTION

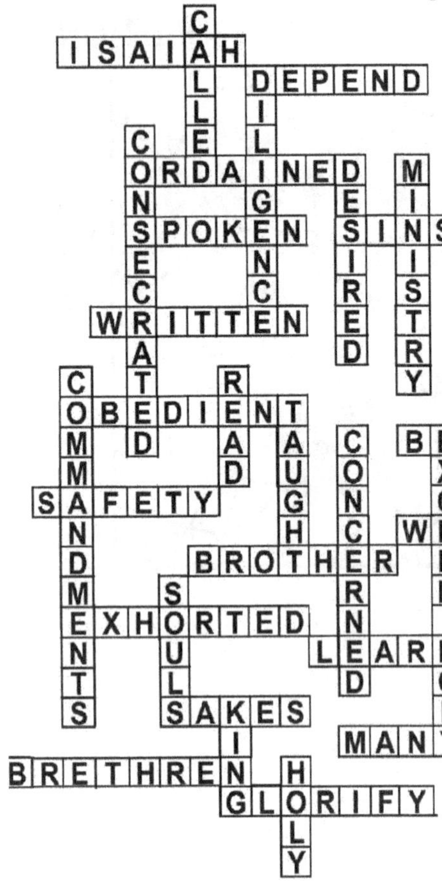

Messiah Will Come

Page 69

SOLUTION

Using the grid coordinates, plot each letter into the correct place and you will see a message.

A: 2B, 5J, 6D, 7H, 8B, 10C
E: 1B, 2F, 3E, 4H, 5G, 6C, 7C, 8H, 9C, 9H, 10H, 10K, 10M,
I: 1E, 2D, 3B, 5A, 10J, 11A, 11E
0: 4D, 5E, 6I, 8F
U: 4A
B: 10G
C: 8E
D: 5L, 8A
F: 2E, 3G
G: 6A, 6G
H: 1A, 3A, 4G, 7B, 7G, 8J, 9B, 9G, 10B, 11D
L:1F, 1G, 3F, 6H, 10D, 10E, 10I
M: 2A, 3C, 4I, 8G, 11F,
N: 2C, 4B, 5B, 5K, 7D, 9D, 11B
P: 5D
R: 5H, 6B, 6J
S; 2G, 3D, 10A
T: 2H, 4C, 4F, 6E, 7F, 7I, 8I, 9F
V: 10L
W: 1D, 5F, 7A, 9A
Y: 6K, 8C, 9I

	A	B	C	D	E	F	G	H	I	J	K	L	M
1	H	E		W	I	L	L						
2	M	A	N	I	F	E	S	T					
3	H	I	M	S	E	L	F						
4	U	N	T	O		T	H	E	M				
5	I	N		P	O	W	E	R		A	N	D	
6	G	R	E	A	T		G	L	O	R	Y		
7	W	H	E	N		T	H	A	T				
8	D	A	Y		C	O	M	E	T	H			
9	W	H	E	N		T	H	E	Y				
10	S	H	A	L	L		B	E	L	I	E	V	E
11	I	N		H	I	M							

Kings Shall Be Thy Nursing Fathers

Page 68

SOLUTION

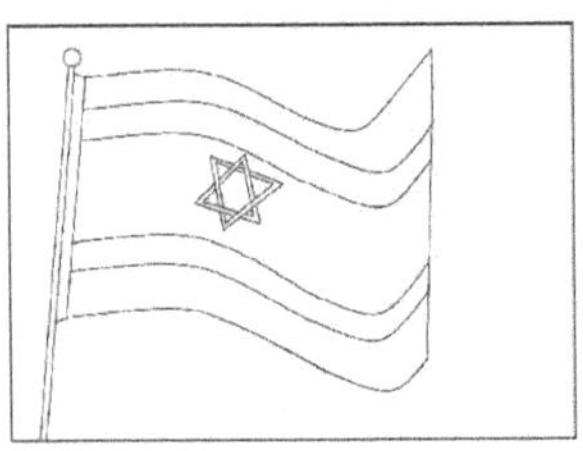

Cross out all the following to see a message:
A and I in EVEN numbered COLUMNS
P except on the 2nd ROW
S except on the last ROW
R on all EVEN numbered ROWS
W on all the ODD numbered ROWS
S in COLUMN 5
R in COLUMN 13 and 17
N in column 4
and all these: J K Q U V X Y Z

1	2	3	4	5	6	7	8	9	10	11	12	13	14	15	16	17	18	19	20	21	22	23	24	
F	V	O	Z	J	W	R	P	U	I	K	Y	T	Z	U	Q	H	J	Q	A	P	E	V	X	1
Y	P	R	E	X	A	S	K	O	R	P	A	L	S	E	Q	X	O	K	Z	F	R	Q	T	2
Z	U	H	I	W	E	V	J	Q	X	Y	L	W	O	V	A	W	R	J	S	Z	D	K	A	3
W	S	X	Y	A	K	R	S	I	V	Q	U	S	J	S	I	P	T	U	R	F	S	J	O	4
R	V	T	A	P	W	U	H	K	A	W	E	R	C	W	Q	R	A	S	O	Y	M	P	V	5
I	Q	J	N	Q	X	P	G	Z	R	J	O	P	Z	F	R	Y	T	Z	Q	X	P	H	J	6
Z	E	P	Y	S	I	M	U	Y	E	J	I	X	S	S	X	P	V	I	K	A	I	W	H	7

FOR THE PEOPLE OF THE LORD WAIT FOR THE COMING OF THE MESSIAH

I WILL COMFORT HER WASTE PLACES

Page 70

2 Nephi 8:3

Can you find a button, candle, 2 deer, eggs and bacon, spoon, brush, knife, key, fish

SOLUTION

They Shall Come to Zion

Page 71

SOLUTION

Christ:

Pleadeth the C A U (S) E of his people

Laid the F O U N D (A) T I O N of the earth

Brings everlasting joy and H O (L) I N E S S

Righteousness shall be F O R E (V) E R

The Lord thy M (A) K E R

Made the D E P (T) H S of the sea a way for the ransomed to pass over

They shall O B T A (I) N gladness

Have covered thee with the S H A D (O) W of mine hand

Sorrow and M O U R (N) I N G shall flee away

The word is Christ's great gift to us:

S A L V A T I O N

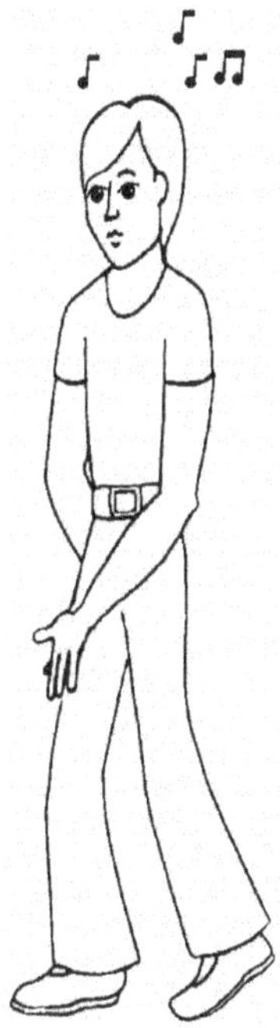

The Spirit and the Body

Page 73

SOLUTION

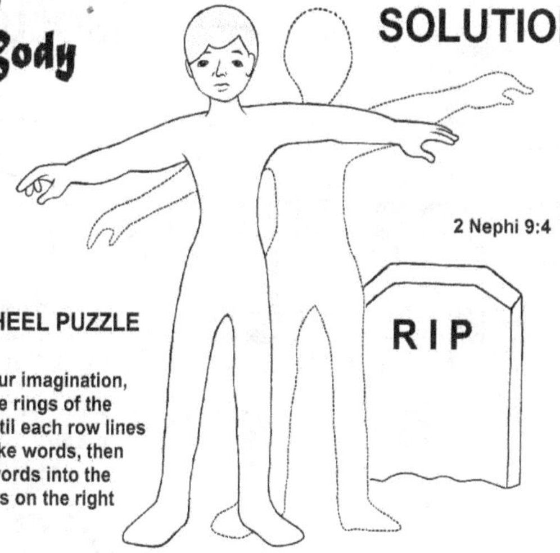

SPINWHEEL PUZZLE

Using your imagination, "spin" the rings of the wheel until each row lines up to make words, then put the words into the sentences on the right side.

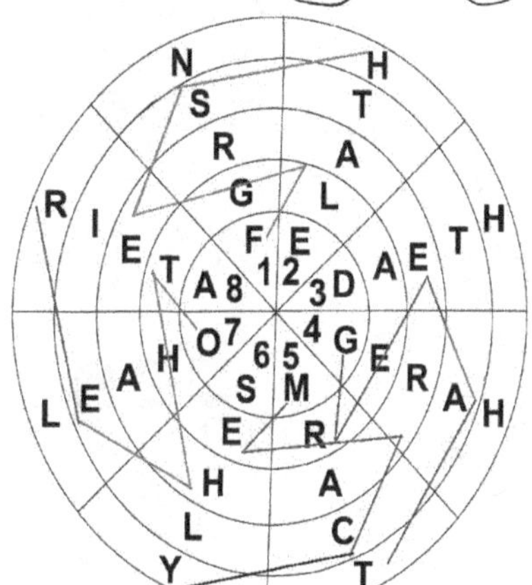

All 1. FLESH
on 2. EARTH
suffers
3. DEATH
but by God's
4. GREAT
5. MERCY
we 6. SHALL
see each
7. OTHER
8. AGAIN

HE WILL COME IN THE BODY

Page 72

SOLUTION

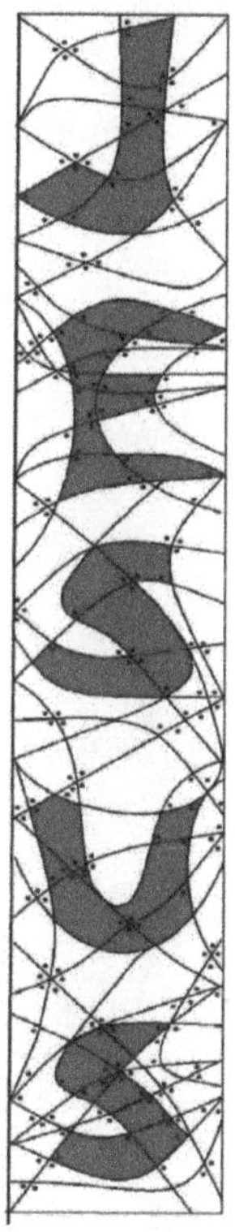

WORDFALL

W	H	E	R	E	F	O	R	E		I	T		M	U	S	T		
N	E	E	D	S		B	E		A	N								
I	N	F	I	N	I	T	E		A	T	O	N	E	M	E	N	T	

Day of Judgment

Page 74 Solution

A	L	P	S	S	E	N	I	L	O	H	J	O	Y	E
G	D	R	E	S	U	R	R	E	C	T	I	O	N	E
N	E	E	H	R	E	P	E	N	T	A	S	O	H	M
I	Z	P	L	T	L	N	M	R	E	H	T	N	T	A
T	I	A	I	I	E	M	T	E	I	S	N	U	E	N
S	T	R	V	M	V	D	X	A	M	F	I	H	D	O
A	P	E	E	A	M	E	N	I	E	S	A	T	N	I
L	A	D	T	Y	C	O	R	E	T	R	S	E	A	T
R	B	R	H	U	E	B	R	E	C	P	G	R	M	A
E	R	E	T	S	N	O	M	T	T	S	E	E	M	D
V	N	E	C	I	T	S	U	J	A	H	A	F	O	N
E	T	G	O	D	E	L	L	I	F	L	U	F	C	U
H	T	T	A	E	S	T	N	E	M	G	D	U	J	O
R	I	G	H	T	E	O	U	S	N	E	S	S	●	F

2 Nephi 9:26

SOLUTION

For the puzzle at right - When you see the arrow, draw a line to the triangle like this: When you see a an asterisk, draw a circle around it like this: When you a diamond, draw a partial circle I ike this:

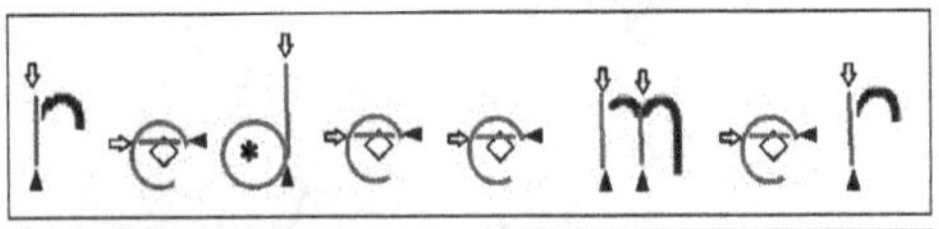

W H E R E T H E R E I S N O

L A W G I V E N T H E R E

I S N O P U N I S H M E N T

Figure out what the message above says by using the Code Key at right

THIS IS THE CODE KEY

A B C D E F

G H I J K

L M N O P

Q R S T U

V W X Y Z